*A Devotional Daybook*
*by Neva Coyle*

# Making Sense of Pain and Struggle

🐞 🐞 🐞 🐞 🐞 🐞 🐞 🐞 🐞 🐞 🐞

Finding the
Strength to
Go On

**BETHANY HOUSE PUBLISHERS**
MINNEAPOLIS, MINNESOTA 55438

Published by Bethany House Publishers
A Ministry of Bethany Fellowship, Inc.
6820 Auto Club Road, Minneapolis, Minnesota 55438

Printed in the United States of America

**Library of Congress Cataloging-in-Publication Data**

Coyle, Neva, 1943–
    Making sense of pain and struggle / Neva Coyle.
        p.   cm.  —  (A Devotional daybook)

    1. Devotional exercises.  2. Consolation.
I. Title.  II. Series: Coyle, Neva, 1943–      Devotional daybook.
BV4832.2.C679   1992
242'.4—dc20                                                        92–31394
ISBN 1–55661–276–1                                                 CIP

To Judy

NEVA COYLE is Founder of Overeaters Victorious and President of Neva Coyle Ministries. Her ministry is enhanced by her bestselling books, tapes, and teaching seminars. Neva and her husband make their home in California.

She may be contacted at:

P.O. Box 2330
Orange, CA 92669

# Preface

I AM AN OVERCOMER. I am destined to be an overcomer. Just as important, I have made a commitment to be an overcomer.

I've fought my share of battles—maybe more than my share. I've struggled with temptation, bad habits, and poor attitudes. I've had disappointment, emotional pain, and enough discouragement to last me my entire lifetime. Come to think of it, I'm fighting a battle or two right now, and there is no doubt I'll face more battles before it's over.

But I have a plan—and that is to *win*. I'm going to overcome every obstacle and win over every discouraging situation I'll ever encounter. I don't consider myself "special," just determined. And I'm not the first, nor am I the last whose destiny is to overcome. It's your destiny, too.

Moses was destined to overcome his stammering tongue. Jonah overcame an unwilling attitude. Daniel and the three Hebrew children overcame oppression and survived a walk through an incinerator. Esther and David were overcomers, and both saved their nation from enemy oppression. Peter dealt with a bad temper; Paul lived with a thorn in the flesh. The example of all these men and women gives us all such hope.

There are present-day overcomers, too, like Joni Eareckson Tada and Dave Roever, two of my heroes. And there are many others: Lucia, a friend whose pastor husband left her for another woman; Mandy, who was abused as a child and has fought her way through to balanced living and emotional health.

Struggling for many years with my weight, I lived with the idea that to win was to get rid of whatever it was I was struggling with—for me that meant to get thin. But I have finally learned this lesson: to overcome does not always mean that we get rid of the problem, but that we press on in spite of it.

Have you ever made any of the following statements?

"I'm ready to give up. I never get what I want."

"This financial problem is destroying what little faith I had."

"I've been so sick for so long, I no longer pray for healing."

"I'm so confused, I don't know which way to turn or who to believe anymore."

"I've been so hurt, I can't trust anyone."

"Disappointment is so heavy, I can't even pray."

If you have thought or said any or all of the above, this book is for you. Here you'll find six of the most important strategies you'll ever need to overcome the obstacles in your life. With each strategy are five daily devotional thoughts for you to personalize.

When you finish this study, you will have learned spiritual strategies that will help you for the rest of your life. They will help you to make sense of your pain and struggle. They will provide you with the strength you need to go on—and more than that, to be an *overcomer!*

# How to Use This Book

THIS DEVOTIONAL STUDY is designed to fit easily into a busy schedule. It is divided into six sections, with five entries in each section. If an entry is read each day, it will take just thirty days to complete the book. Take a few minutes each day to read the suggested Scripture reference and accompanying thoughts. The questions at the end of each entry will help you focus on a personal application of the Scripture selection.

If the book is used in a group study, members should study the five entries of a section during the week and then meet as a group to discuss the material. In this way the book will take six weeks to complete, or longer depending on the needs of the group. It is also easily adaptable to a ministry group that is already established or a Sunday school class.

If you are using this material in a group study, suggested guidelines and discussion questions are included at the end of the book for the use of the leader.

# Devotional Daybooks
## By Neva Coyle

*Making Sense of Pain and Struggle*
*Meeting the Challenges of Change*
*A New Heart . . . A New Start*

# Contents

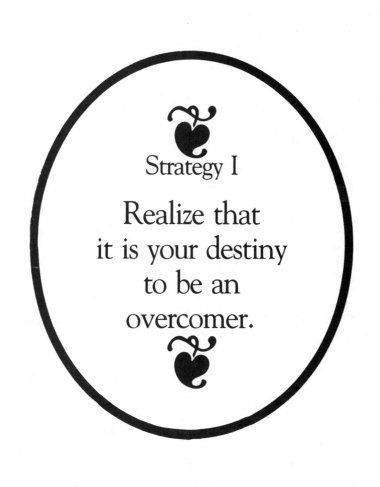

### Strategy I

Realize that
it is your destiny
to be an
overcomer.

*For* we are God's workmanship, created in Christ Jesus to do good works, which God prepared in advance for us to do.

EPHESIANS 2:10

YOU HAVE DECIDED not to give up. Perhaps you bought this book in the hope of finding the strength you need to go on and to make sense out of your struggle and pain.

I know how you feel. I have struggled through much pain. I've wondered if God could change me or use me. I have battled temptations and fought with discouragement that once threatened to ruin my life and the organization I built to help other strugglers.

At a time when life seemed so bleak and my future was in question, I decided to return to what I understood to be the basis of the Christian life—my identity in Christ.

At the heart of that identity rests the destiny of every Christian—and that is to live the life of an overcomer.

As I began to understand five distinct spiritual principles, my struggle began to make sense. I was able to put my pain in perspective, and joy and strength returned.

These principles form the basis for the first strategy for successfully living the Christian life.

Chapter
· 1 ·

Destined for
Relationship

*"Yet to all who received him, to those who believed in his name, he gave the right to become children of God . . ."*

John 1:12

And God stepped out in space
    And He looked around and said,
"I'm lonely. I'll make me a world."
    As far as the eye of God could see
Darkness covered everything.
    Darker than a hundred midnights
Down in a cypress swamp. . . .

Was James Weldon Johnson right? Could God be lonely? Did the one perfect, complete, eternal Being create you and me to fill that loneliness?

I don't know if God was lonely before I came into His life, but this I do know: I was lonely before I asked Him to enter mine.

Johnson's poem "The Creation" attempts to describe the blackness before God created light. The words he uses describe the darkness, the hopelessness of life without Christ.

God created physical light by setting the sun in our sky. But creating *spiritual light* required more than His creativity, it demanded His sacrifice. And so He came and lived as a man among us. He walked our streets, tasted the dust, and tired under the same toil that we do. In so doing, He provided a way for us to live in a relationship with Him.

By sending His Son, Jesus, God the Father gave us spiritual light. He showed that He was willing to give himself. We no longer have to live apart from Him. We each can accept His Son. We believe the fact that He died for our sins, and we enter a loving, personal relationship with our true Savior.

It is amazing that we can know Him. It is even more amazing that a relationship with God is the destiny of everyone who turns his spirit over to Jesus Christ.

And as if paying the penalty for our sin wasn't enough, God also gave us *sonship*. We don't deserve either, yet both are freely given. By accepting Jesus, we actually become sons and daughters of God, who in His love, " . . . predestined us to be adopted as his sons through Jesus Christ, in accordance with his pleasure and will—to the praise of his glorious grace, which he has freely given us in the One he loves. In him we have redemption through his blood, the forgiveness of sins, in accordance with the riches of God's grace that he lavished on us with all wisdom and understanding" (Ephesians 1:5–8).

As sons and daughters we are now full heirs to the "family" fortune and estate:

"Now if we are children, then we are heirs—heirs of God and co-heirs with Christ" (Romans 8:17).

Designed for relationship with God, destined to sonship in His Son, Jesus. Accepting Him is the first step in the first strategy to becoming an overcomer. It is where all life begins; where eternity begins.

The struggles you and I have are not eternal—but your life in Christ is.

———

Write out a brief paragraph of how you came to accept Christ as your Savior. If you haven't invited Him into your heart, and would like to, write out a simple prayer of invitation.

What are some of the struggles in your life in which you need help overcoming?

How do sons and daughters of God approach problems differ-ently than those who have no relationship with Him?

What is your destiny as one of God's children?

Chapter
· 2 ·

Destined to Be
Like Christ

*"For those God foreknew he also predestined to be
conformed to the likeness of his Son, that he might be the
firstborn among many brothers."*

Romans 8:29

I WISH YOU could see my grandchildren. As a typical grandmother, I think they are wonderful, intelligent, and charming.

The amazing thing about them is the remarkable "minia-
tures" they are of my own children. My two granddaughters
are almost mirror-images of my two daughters at the same age.
I carry a picture of my daughter Sandra at nine months, next
to one of her daughter Alexis at the same age. People who
patiently humor me by looking at my "Grandma's album" are
not usually aware that they are looking at two different babies.

Because our family was built through adoption as well as
natural birth, family resemblance is a delightful phenomenon.
None of my children resemble one another.

I have noticed the same to be true in God's family. Related
by adoption through the new-birth experience makes us family, but none of us resembles the other—at least not on the
outside. Our relationship comes through His blood that was
shed for us, blood that covers our sin.

In time, we do grow to be more like each other—though in fact it is Jesus who we are growing more to be like. You and I have been destined to be conformed—to fit, as it were, into the image of Christ.

Strange as it may seem, even our struggles and our pain can help us to reach this destiny. Let me illustrate:

Amy Carmichael, a missionary to India, relates the story of a village goldsmith who was refining ore. He heated it until it was in liquid form, then heated it even hotter to burn out every impurity. Observing that the liquid gold seemed pure, someone asked, "How hot does it have to get?" "Until I can see my face in it" was the man's reply.

That's the way I think God uses the struggles of my life: They are the heat that brings the impurities to the surface. God does not *cause* the struggles in my life, but He can use them—if I allow Him to.

The struggles I've experienced have brought out in me bad attitudes, unforgiveness, selfishness, pride. The pain of those struggles has motivated me to seek Christ at a deeper level. They have drawn me closer to His Word and to His principles for living. My problems have often been the very thing that has given me more compassion, patience, and tolerance with others who are struggling.

I want to look like Jesus. Not like my friends and co-workers—but like Him. I want to think of God carrying a picture of me next to one of Jesus and saying, "See how she resembles Him? She is a mirror-image of Jesus."

---

Think of someone that you resemble. In what ways are you like that person?

In what ways do you think you are more like Christ than you were several years ago—or months ago?




In what ways do you want to be more like Him?

## Chapter · 3 ·

## Destined to Produce Fruit

*"I am the vine; you are the branches. If a man remains in me and I in him, he will bear much fruit."*

John 15:5

DID YOU KNOW that you were destined to be productive? To accomplish great things? It's hard to believe that when it seems the whole world is out to prove just the opposite.

In today's complex world it is easy to feel useless. We are overwhelmed by artificial intelligence, pressured by busy schedules, and wounded by cultural prejudice, making us feel inadequate and isolated.

A middle-aged secretary can feel threatened by the technology of word processors and spreadsheet software. A woman returning to the workforce in her late forties or fifties faces a cash register that *beeps* at her when she makes a mistake, announcing it to everyone in the store. . . .

Being a Christian should make a difference. Why, then, does being a Christian sometimes make the struggle seem worse? I believe, first of all, it is because a person who belongs to Christ is out-of-step with the sinful world. Add to that the world's devaluation of human life, and our feelings of inadequacy seem to multiply. This battle is only won by laying hold of the truth of God's Word.

A person passed over for a promotion needs to remind herself: "I didn't choose Jesus, He chose me. Not only that, He has appointed me that I go and bear fruit. This job is not the only place where I can do that. I'll ask God to show me where I was designed to bear fruit. I need this job—but only to provide for my needs while I bear fruit for God's kingdom."

"You did not choose me, but I chose you and appointed you to go and bear fruit—fruit that will last. Then the Father will give you whatever you ask in my name" (John 15:16).

When you are overcome by feelings of worthlessness and defeat, let God breathe new life into you by telling yourself this truth: "No matter what I've done or what I've been, *because of Jesus*, I now have the ability to live a life worthy of the Lord. I may not be able to please anyone else, but I can please Him. I can bear the fruit of good work. I am growing in the knowledge of God."

"And we pray this in order that you may live a life worthy of the Lord and may please him in every way: bearing fruit in every good work, growing in the knowledge of God, being strengthened with all power according to his glorious might so that you may have great endurance and patience, and joyfully giving thanks to the father, who has qualified you to share in the inheritance of the saints in the kingdom of light" (Colossians 1:10–12).

Today, begin to experience the wonder of the fruitful life: This is your destiny. You were designed to be fruitful, because you have been attached—grafted in to the vine, Jesus. You now draw your strength and worth from Him. His life pulses through your veins, giving you energy and worth. He provides one hundred percent of the nourishment you need to be productive and fruitful.

Why settle for mere survival when you can overcome? Let this be the turning point of your life.

---

When was the last time you let yourself hurt with a person in pain?

When was the last time you prayed *with* someone instead of promising to pray *for* them?

Look around your circle of friends and name those whom you have influenced to think about Jesus.

Look into the faces of the people you come in contact with every day—are there non-Christians among them? If not, how can you meet some?

# Chapter · 4 ·

## Destined for Victory

*"With God we will gain the victory, and he will trample down our enemies."*

Psalm 60:12

A YOUNG BOY NAMED DAVID was sent by his father to the frontlines of a battle his brothers were fighting. He was sent to take food and to bring back a report: a simple assignment, but one that led him to a great destiny. For it was in this situation that David realized his destiny as a victor.

We know the story: David knocked out the harassing Goliath with a simple stone expertly flung between the giant's eyes, then cut off his head with a sword.

How was it that this shepherd boy was more courageous than the entire Israeli army? I believe his courage came from knowing a mighty truth.

It is the same truth that keeps Don Wildmon fighting pornography, Pat Robertson fighting for national right-eousness, and Operation Rescue fighting our national dis-grace—the murder of our unborn children.

It is the same truth that motivates missionaries to move into unreached people groups that are gripped by spiritual darkness, and motivates Christian teachers to move into the inner city to work in crime-ridden public schools. It is the same powerful truth that keeps pastors in their pulpits and Sunday school teachers in their classrooms. This truth will also help you find and live out your victorious destiny.

David stated it in simple, yet powerful words: "You come against me with sword and spear and javelin, but I come against you in the name of the LORD Almighty . . . it is not by sword or spear that the LORD saves; for the battle is the LORD'S, and he will give all of you into our hands" (1 Samuel 17:45–47).

Whatever we face, we can go in the name of the Lord. Whatever threatens, whatever challenges, whatever defies us will have to reckon with God. The battle is His, and the victory is ours.

The Bible is full of promises of victory:

"He holds victory in store for the upright, he is a shield to those whose walk is blameless, for he guards the course of the just and protects the way of his faithful ones" (Proverbs 2:7–8).

"Who shall separate us from the love of Christ? Shall trouble or hardship or persecution or famine or nakedness or danger or sword? As it is written: 'For your sake we face death all day long; we are considered as sheep to be slaughtered.' No, in all these things we are more than conquerors through him who loved us" (Romans 8:35–37).

Remember: While we are assured that the battle is the Lord's, we are not spared from the battle. There can be no victory without it. But the promise of God's presence and power goes with us and gives us courage.

When we are in Jesus—living in His will, abiding in His Word—we are victors. Before the battle begins, the outcome is sure. No matter how difficult the struggle, how lopsided the score sheet, the *winner* has been determined and the trophy engraved before the contest begins.

---

Will you accept your destiny as a victorious person?

If you knew you could not fail, what would you attempt?

What victories have you seen in your struggles? Knowing that victory belongs to the people of God, how should that knowledge affect our definition of what looks like defeat?

If you were to announce confidently, "The victory is mine in the name of the Lord," what struggle would you be addressing?

If you could remember to say, "It's not over till it's over," how would that change the way you approach your problems?

Chapter
· 5 ·

Becoming
Unshakable

> *"But thanks be to God! He gives us the victory through
> our Lord Jesus Christ. Therefore, my dear brothers,
> stand firm. Let nothing move you."*
>
> 1 Corinthians 15:57–58

MILLIONS WATCHED ON TV the recent devastation in
Los Angeles. All of southern California, living in preparation
for a major earthquake, was not prepared for the tragedy of
the racially inspired riots.

Men and women of reason cried out for control, but they
were ignored by the looters. Leaders promised reform, but were
shouted down by hecklers. Celebrities risked their own safety
to enter the area set afire to show their support for a peaceful
means of change. Inner-city ministries and missions became
more deluged with the homeless and hungry than ever before.

Regardless of the incident that triggered the riots, sin went
on a rampage in Los Angeles on May 1, 1992. The forces of
hell are always looking for an excuse, and even legitimate
causes can be exploited by evil.

Big cities are not the only hotbeds of wickedness waiting
to be unleashed. Small towns can be also, as well as individual
lives.

Sinful attitudes, pain turned to bitterness, and a general lack of love and concern for others all surface in our own churches and families. The devastation may not make it to the morning headlines or the evening newscast, but the pain is written on the faces of those who are wounded by it.

Discouragement, disillusionment, and defeat mark the lives of those who have not learned that their destiny is to be steadfast, regardless of their circumstances.

*Stand firm*, God's Word says. *Let nothing move you.*

The Evil One would unleash his fury against you. His goal is to cause you to abandon your belief in a heavenly destiny. But we know who we are; we know that victory is ours; we know that, while we may fight the battle, the Lord has given us the victory. *Therefore, we will not be shaken!*

---

When are you the most tempted to quit or give up?

What do you say to yourself when you experience a temporary setback?

How do you find the courage to get up again when you have failed?

In what areas are you shakable?

In what areas are you unshakable?

How are you more aware of your destiny to overcome after completing these five studies?

In which of these areas do you want to see more evidence of Christ's presence and power:

    1. My relationship with Him

    2. My relationships with others

3. Fruitfulness


4. Victorious living


5. Being unshakable

Strategy II

Set yourself for
the long battle.

Not that I have already obtained all this, or have already been made perfect, but I press on to take hold of that for which Christ Jesus took hold of me. Brothers, I do not consider myself yet to have taken hold of it. But one thing I do: Forgetting what is behind and straining toward what is ahead, I press on toward the goal to win the prize for which God has called me heavenward in Christ Jesus.

PHILIPPIANS 3:12–14

IT'S SO EASY TO BE CAUGHT in the mind-set that we should, we *must*, get everything we want in as little time and with as little effort as possible. Credit cards are offered in the mail without solicitation, restaurant chains offer lunch in ten minutes or there is no charge, advertisements promise quick weight loss with no restrictive dieting or strenuous exercise, direct-mail campaigns sell everything you want from questionable health products to shoes in hard-to-find sizes—easy shopping from your recliner chair. Electronically distributed information can make the daily newspaper almost obsolete before it's delivered.

No wonder advertising slogans and promises include words like: *instant, in no time at all, it's a piece of cake, so easy a child can do it,* and *it's never been easier.* . . .

These promises appeal to us in the midst of our busy lives, and make the thought of waiting and working toward a goal seem hopeless and outdated.

Overcoming still involves *work.* The results of disciplining ourselves can be a long time in coming, and the reward may be only in the future. No wonder we fall for the popular preaching that tells us God will perform for us upon command, like an automatic-teller machine at our local bank.

Some things take longer than that. The answers to life's problems are not available through a computer data base. Character is not developed by a snap of God's fingers, but through the working and reworking of a willing heart. That takes effort, patience, commitment. It takes time.

If we are to make some sense of our pain and struggle, we must plan a strategy of overcoming through preparation for the long battle.

# Chapter
## · 6 ·

# A Message for the Mature

*"Brothers, I could not address you as spiritual but as worldly—mere infants in Christ. I gave you milk, not solid food, for you were not yet ready for it. Indeed, you are still not ready."*

1 Corinthians 3:1–2

IN THE PREDAWN DARKNESS, the barracks door flies open and the shrill of the sergeant's whistle splits the air.

"Hit the floor, soldier!" he bellows. "Out of that sack!"

The young, inexperienced soldiers jump to the sergeant's command. They dress quickly, make their beds without a wrinkle, line up, and march to the morning meal. Afterward they line up again and march back. They go on maneuvers and train on the obstacle course. They polish their boots to a high shine, clean their weapons repeatedly, and keep their quarters impeccably neat and spotless. Soldiers in training learn to take orders without question and to work as a unit. The military is not where you find individuality—but where you lose it. The soldier becomes a small part of something much larger than himself—the army.

The Christian is part of God's army. We are soldiers for the Lord. What would happen if the young soldier responded to his sergeant the way many of us respond to God's commands, training, and discipline? Can anyone imagine a soldier saying, "Please don't ask so much of me all at once. I'm just a new soldier"?

We say: "I can't take on the responsibility of teaching a class or tending the nursery, because then I'll be committed to being there all the time. I think going to church should be my choice, not my obligation."

"I don't have the time to be a daily Bible reader unless I get up a little earlier, and I need all the sleep I can get."

"Tithing is an *Old Testament* teaching. It's legalistic. Besides, how do I know the money is being used wisely?"

"Help with an all-church work day? Not me. I work all week, the weekends are mine. That church has plenty of money—let them hire someone to do what needs to be done."

"Write to my congressman about moral issues? Never. I'm not one of those fanatics. He probably doesn't read all those letters anyway."

"Go on a mission trip? That's not my idea of a fun vacation."

"Talk to my co-worker about Jesus? But that would mark me as a target for all the religious jokes."

Hold it right there, soldier. This is God's army. If you were called up for an on-the-spot inspection, what areas would need more work? As the old question goes, if you were accused of being a Christian would there be enough evidence to make the charge stick?

We are all in training. Not "in case" we go to war—God's army *is* at war!

"For our struggle is not against flesh and blood, but against the rulers, against the authorities, against the powers of this dark world and against the spiritual forces of evil in the heavenly realms" (Ephesians 6:12).

We are all on duty, every hour of every day, every place we go. We must be dressed in uniform and completely armed at all times.

"Therefore put on the full armor of God, so that when the day of evil comes, you may be able to stand your ground, and after you have done everything, to stand. Stand firm then, with the belt of truth buckled around your waist, with the breastplate of righteousness in place, and with your feet fitted with the readiness that comes from the gospel of peace. In addition to all this, take up the shield of faith, with which you can extinguish all the flaming arrows of the evil one. Take the helmet of salvation and the sword of the Spirit, which is the word of God. And pray in the Spirit on all occasions with all kinds of prayers and requests. With this in mind, be alert and always keep on praying for all the saints" (Ephesians 6:13–18).

Our mission requires the very latest in spiritual warfare technology.

"The weapons we fight with are not the weapons of the world. On the contrary, they have divine power to demolish strongholds" (2 Corinthians 10:4).

We know our target, and we're fully informed about our enemy.

"We demolish arguments and every pretension that sets itself up against the knowledge of God, and we take captive every thought to make it obedient to Christ" (2 Corinthians 10:5).

There is no such thing as "boot camp" in God's army. Once you are born again, you find yourself immediately in the trenches. It's time to switch from milk to meat. Time to leave behind the excuses we sometimes use to stay immature and irresponsible. It's time to continue growing.

We grow when we allow ourselves to be trained by pain and struggle. We will find the strength to go on because we have chosen to learn how to become overcomers.

Instead of defending ourselves with excuses when we make mistakes we choose to face them, to admit them, and to grow because of them. We used to shift blame, but no longer. Now we can take full responsibility for our shortcomings because we know God has accepted us already.

We admit we need prayer and counseling to overcome damage to our souls. We courageously seek out companionship with those older and wiser, for mentoring and guidance. We place ourselves at risk by volunteering for new ministry assignments rather than stagnating in our comfort zones.

You see we have a plan, you and I. We plan not only to make it through God's military academy—but we plan to graduate with honors. We won't be wearing the traditional four-cornered graduation cap—we'll be wearing the overcomer's crown!

———————

When is it most tempting for you to use the "baby Christian" excuse?

Recall an experience when you overcame a temptation. How did that change you?

What is the hardest part of becoming mature?

Which piece of God's armor do you find still doesn't quite fit you yet? (Ephesians 6:10–18)

# Chapter
## · 7 ·

## Are We There Yet?

> *"For the revelation awaits an appointed time; it speaks of the end and will not prove false. Though it linger, wait for it; it will certainly come and will not delay."*
>
> Habakkuk 2:3

"ARE WE THERE YET?" wails the impatient five-year-old from the backseat.

We know from reading the recipe that it takes eighteen minutes for muffins to bake. The travel agent tells us it takes about six hours to fly from coast to coast. We know from experience how long it takes to get home from our place of work, and we can approximate how long it takes to get a haircut.

But some things can't be measured by minutes or a target date circled on the calendar. For example, we have no way of knowing when certain realities of life will sink into our children's minds, or when they will be ready to be on their own. Some women wait and pray for "Mr. Right." We wait for "the other shoe to drop" or for "our ship to come in." Many of us know what it's like waiting for the phone to ring, or for the results of a medical test to come in.

There is one more area we wish we could predict, and that

is our spiritual maturity. It's so tempting to go to God and ask, "Am I there yet?"

Have you ever called out to God, in the misery of a personal crisis, "I can't take any more!"

Have you ever wondered how long it takes to become an overcomer?

It takes as long as it takes—and that is a lifetime: a lifetime of wounds and scars; a lifetime scarred by sin and renewed by grace; a lifetime of joys mixed with sorrows; of learning and struggling to learn more; of replacing doubt with faith, error with truth, and bad habits with good discipline.

But the overcomer's life is touched with mercy, motivated by grace, covered with love. It is seasoned with self-control, and held together with the promises of God.

Are we there yet? No. But we're getting there! And we know that while we have some distance to go, we *will* get there—even if it takes all the time that God allows us here on earth.

"[We are] confident of this, that he who began a good work in you will carry it on to completion until the day of Christ Jesus" (Philippians 1:6).

---

When are you tempted to give up?

How much time have you been given to become an overcomer?

Which excites you the most:
  Being a triumphant Christian
  Becoming an overcomer

What is the difference between the two?

Chapter
· 8 ·

Surviving the
Ups and
Downs

*"My soul is in anguish. How long, O LORD,
how long?"*

Psalm 6:3

DAVID KNEW DEFEAT long before he knew victory. He knew sorrow before he knew joy. He knew well what we would call the "ups and downs" of life when he penned this prayer:

"How long, O LORD? Will you forget me forever? How long will you hide your face from me? How long must I wrestle with my thoughts and every day have sorrow in my heart? How long will my enemy triumph over me? Look on me and answer, O LORD, my God. Give light to my eyes, or I will sleep in death; my enemy will say, 'I have overcome him,' and my foes will rejoice when I fall" (Psalm 13:1–4).

This was written long before David wrote the following words of praise:

"I will praise you as long as I live, and in your name I will lift up my hands. My soul will be satisfied as with the richest of foods; with singing lips my mouth will praise you. On my bed I remember you; I think of you through the watches of the night. Because you are my help, I sing in the shadow of your wings. My soul clings to you; your right hand upholds me. They who seek my life will be destroyed; they will go down to the depths of the earth" (Psalm 63:4–9).

What made the difference in David's life? He learned to navigate the *downs* and climb the *ups* of life. And so can you. You can survive the ups and downs when you put the following principles to work in your character:

1. *Offer sacrifices of praise.*

"Through Jesus, therefore, let us continually offer to God a sacrifice of praise—the fruit of lips that confess his name" (Hebrews 13:15).

Sacrifices of praise are not emotionally based, they are *purpose based*. Praise that is offered outside of feelings or circumstances does not depend on emotional motivation. We don't praise God because we *feel* like it, we praise Him for one reason only—because He is worthy.

2. *Learn to be still.*

"Be still before the LORD and wait patiently for him" (Psalm 37:7).

It is tempting to lament over our emotional roller coaster experiences—to keep telling God in detail how needy we are, and how He should answer our prayers.

Yes, there are times when we need to spill our hearts—every fear, every doubt, every need. But when that is done, it is time to remain in prayer—waiting patiently before God.

In my experience, it is then that the comfort and strength come.

3. *Walk in His ways.*

"Yes, LORD, walking in the way of your laws, we wait for you; your name and renown are the desire of our hearts" (Isaiah 26:8).

How tempting it is to think that walking in His ways isn't getting us anywhere. Isn't it more accurate to say that walking in His ways isn't getting us where *we want to go*? It is important to keep on practicing the principles of God's Word, no matter what. Forgiving, loving, praying, praising, worshiping—not because we feel like it, but because we choose His Word above our feelings.

43

### 4. Don't give up hope.

"The LORD is good to those whose hope is in him, to the one who seeks him" (Lamentations 3:25).

Our hope is not in a hopeless god. Our God is full of promise, life, and hope. Our hope is not in answered prayers or changed circumstances, but in God who can change our heart and give us a changed life!

### 5. Trust in God.

"I will wait for the LORD . . . I will put my trust in him" (Isaiah 8:17).

"Some trust in chariots and some in horses, but we trust in the name of the LORD our God. They are brought to their knees and fall, but we rise up and stand firm" (Psalm 20:7).

No matter how black the moment, how depressing the outlook, or how bad the news, you can trust in God. When everyone else proves to be untrustworthy, He remains trustworthy. No matter who has betrayed you, He never will. Though you have been ridiculed and abused, you can trust God to affirm and heal. He can be trusted with the deepest secrets and most precious desires. He never calls your important issues and dreams trivial. No one can be trusted like God—in fact, no one can be fully trusted *but* God.

### 6. Speak truth to yourself.

"I say to myself, 'The LORD is my portion; therefore I will wait for him' " (Lamentations 3:24).

The world is full of lies and deceit. God's Word is full of truth and light. The world will tell you you are worth nothing; God's Word tells you your worth is secured by the life of His Son. The world tells you you are unloved; God tells you He loved you enough to send His Son, Jesus, to walk in the places you walk, to feel the feelings you feel, and ultimately to give His life for your sins. Tell yourself these truths. Speak them to yourself often.

### 7. Enter into worship.

"Ascribe to the LORD, O families of nations, ascribe to the LORD glory and strength, ascribe to the LORD the glory due his name. Bring an offering and come before him; worship the LORD in the splendor of his holiness" (1 Chronicles 16:28–29).

Don't wait for the Lord's Day. Worship Him today! Don't wait for someone to lead you into worship; enter it on your own. Sing praises to God; use words of praise you never used before. Speak words of love to Him and draw close to Him. *Worship* is the way. *This* is the time.

Following these seven principles will give you a smoother course, a straight path. They will add strength and consistency to your daily life. They will give you new perspective in dealing with your personal pain and struggle.

———————

Which of the seven principles is the easiest for you? Why?

Which is the most difficult? Why?

Speaking God's truth in your most difficult circumstances may require some study and further research of God's Word. How can you do that?

Who is a good person to ask for help in searching out a biblical answer to a particular problem?

# Chapter · 9 ·

## 🍂 Patiently Waiting 🍂

*"I waited patiently for the LORD; he turned to me and heard my cry."*

Psalm 40:1

"WITHIN 30 DAYS, you could be. . . ."

"It's *fast* acting."

"This works immediately."

"Fast results are guaranteed with this product."

"You will have instant results, we promise."

Sound familiar? You read the slogans every day in magazines and newspapers. You listen to them on TV and radio: advertising slogans that promise the end of waiting. It's the modern way; it's the American way. We want things now, not later.

Living only for the moment requires that we have within easy reach every push-button convenience. We want to live without any delays, and many of us lose the ability to wait.

But patient waiting is an investment in the future. It gives us hope for today *and* hope for tomorrow.

When you set your mind on winning the war you are agreeing to wait through all the struggles to come to victory.

Look in your Bible. The pages are filled with stories of

people who grew while they waited.

For Moses, it was a long time between the burning bush experience and the Red Sea crossing.

Consider Abraham: How long was it between the promise of a multitude of descendants and the birth of his son?

Job waited long for restoration. Esther waited for an opportunity. Hannah waited for a baby boy. The prophetess Anna waited most of her life for the promised Messiah.

Waiting patiently brings bountiful benefits. Once we get our impatience under control we can begin to receive those benefits.

Waiting is hoping, and hoping helps us wait with patience (Romans 8:25).

The Holy Spirit's work within us while we are waiting produces patience (Galatians 5:22).

Patiently waiting produces results—not only in that we receive what was promised, but it spares us from the pressure of having to produce results by self-effort (Hebrews 6:13–15).

Making sense of pain and struggle takes time and great patience. It requires that many of us learn to wait. But patiently waiting can become our defense against anxiety. When we decide to take the giant step toward maturity by *waiting*, we are released from the pressure of instant gratification.

We begin to add new words and phrases to our vocabulary, like *consider*, *think it over*, and *think it through*. We find ourselves willing to take time to pray and to get counsel before we make major decisions. We begin to look toward the future, full of hope and expectation while free of impulse and selfish demands. We discover a spontaneity in worship and the freedom of uninhibited laughter because we suffer less from the pain of hasty decisions gone sour.

James said, "We consider blessed those who have persevered. You have heard . . . and have seen what the Lord finally brought about" (James 5:11).

Some day, we too will see God's promises fulfilled in our lives.

We are no longer in a hurry. We become more aware of living with an eternal dimension in our relationship with God. We lose our need for selfish demands and embrace instead the urgency of kingdom matters.

And then—just when we think it will never happen—we discover a promise whose time has come.

And what's more, we're ready for it!

———

How hard is it for you to wait?

What emotional signals do you receive from others who do not want to wait?

What emotional signals do you send to others when you do not want to wait?

When have you had no choice but to wait?

What positive change is taking place in you while you are waiting?




How else would you *like* to learn patience besides waiting?




How else *could* you learn it?

# Keep Your Eyes On the Prize

*"Let your eyes look straight ahead, fix your gaze directly before you."*

Proverbs 4:25

PATIENT PERSISTENCE often spells the difference between success and failure, between satisfaction and disappointment. If we can receive promises by patiently waiting, we can lose them by impatient demands. And I am convinced that we can also lose the fulfillment of what God has promised because, in the waiting, we *forget* the promise.

If you've set your mind for the long battle, chosen to mature by agreeing to the lifelong process of becoming an overcomer; if you've learned to navigate life's ups and downs and become an expert at waiting, you must still add one more principle: *Keep your eye on the prize—the promise.*

Isaiah 46 provides the wonderful process by which we keep our promise of overcoming always before us and the hope of its fulfillment:

"Remember this, fix it in mind, take it to heart, you rebels. Remember the former things, those of long ago; I am God, and there is no other; I am God, and there is none like me. I make known the end from the beginning, from ancient times, what is still to come. I say: My purpose will stand, and I will do all that I please" (Isaiah 46:8–10).

Here are the steps:

## 1. *Remember.*

"Remember the former things, those of long ago" (Isaiah 46:9a).

I was facing one more in a series of major surgeries. It was an operation I needed in order to live, so I had no choice. I was facing some pretty rough days. But I had a spiritual base for the faith I needed in God's Word. And it was the "former things"—things God had already done in my life—that gave me a historical base. My Bible-based faith gave me assurance; my historically based faith gave me comfort.

In the same way, you too can establish a historical as well as a biblical basis for your faith.

## 2. *Fix it in mind.*

"I am God, and there is no other; I am God, and there is none like me. I make known the end from the beginning, from ancient times, what is still to come" (Isaiah 46:9b–10a).

Fear is a dense fog. It can block out the very sunshine of God's identity and power. Unless I willingly take my eyes off overwhelming situations and consciously fix my mind on *who* God is and *what* He is, I lose the war.

You and I cannot predict the outcome. Only God knows the end from the beginning. He knows well the pathway through the middle of terror and conflict. He has full knowledge of the past and a firm hold on the future.

One thing takes more effort, more discipline, than believing God can or will do something: fixing your mind on *Him* while keeping your eye on the promise.

## 3. *Take heart.*

"I say: My purpose will stand, and I will do all that I please" (Isaiah 46:10b).

Parents of wayward sons and daughters—take heart! Wives of unsaved husbands—take heart! Women strapped by financial difficulties—hold on to God! Single mothers—be strong in the Lord! Caregivers of the elderly—wait patiently on God! Cherished one, chained to an addiction—take heart! God has a will for you, a plan for your life. And what's more, He is determined to see it completed.

Let the promise of Isaiah 46:10 be renewed for you.

"My purpose *will* stand. . . ."

"I *will* do. . . ."

---

List three major prayers God has answered for you within the last two years.

List two smaller prayers God has answered for you within the last two months.

List something God has done for you within the last two months that you didn't even ask Him for.

What have you had your mind fixed on before now?

What have you decided to fix it on after this study?

If God were to fulfill *His* purpose for you, using one of your deepest desires, what would that purpose be?

If God were to fulfill His will concerning a major prayer on your heart differently than what you have asked, how would you handle it?

In which ways have you chosen to set yourself for the long battle?
I will stop using the "baby Christian" excuse.
I will stop asking "Am I there yet?"
I will become a patient waiter.
I will keep my eye on the prize.

Strategy III

Understand
the obstacles.

$M$an born of woman is of few days and full of trouble.

JOB 14:1

WE ALL UNDERSTAND what it is to "come up against it"—that is, to experience a hard time.

Obstacles come from many sources. They can come at us from outside sources, such as physical limitations, cultural prejudice, or lack of opportunity. No matter the source, every obstacle, yes *every* one, can serve to teach us God's ways—if we choose the right attitude toward them when they come.

Understanding obstacles can help us make sense of pain and struggle. Overcoming them gives us the strength to go on.

Chapter
· 11 ·

🍀
Dead Ends—
New
Beginnings
🍀

*"When he came to his senses, he said, 'How many of my*
*father's hired men have food to spare, and here I am*
*starving to death! I will set out and go back to my father*
*and say to him: Father, I have sinned against heaven and*
*against you. I am no longer worthy to be called your son;*
*make me like one of your hired men.' So he got up and*
*went to his father."*

Luke 15:17–20

NOT ALL OBSTACLES are put in our way by others; we
create a fair amount of obstacles on our own. Like the prodigal,
we too seek to grab our inheritance and go our own way.
Eventually, though, we end up in a dead-end situation, with
no apparent way out. Worse, we realize that *we* had the major
part in arriving at that situation.

But with every self-made obstacle, we can make a decision
whether or not to "stay stuck."

What did the prodigal son do to escape his dead end? First,
he recognized that he had come to the end of his resources.
He'd gone through his money and his friends. He had nothing
left except himself and a lousy job.

Second, he came to his senses. Reality is pretty rough

sometimes, and a pigpen is a good place to help you come to your senses. The prodigal had a little conversation with himself. The Bible tells us, "He said to himself. . . ." There are times when no matter what anyone else tells us, we aren't willing to change until the problem becomes evident to us. Then we finally "wake up," and *say to ourselves*. . . .

Next, this young man made a decision. "I will set out. . . ." And that was probably the first rational decision he'd made in a long time. We may not have made good decisions about our direction until we actually smack into an obstacle. This irresponsible young man reveals a great deal of wisdom: He did not seek a way *out*, but a way *back*. Often the way to overcome the obstacle of the dead end is to retrace your steps. *How did I get here? Where did I go wrong?*

He also planned his approach. "I will say to my father. . . ." As children, we sometimes conspired together before the folks got home to get the story straight as to how the window got broken. But the young man in our story had no one to confer with. *I'd better come right out and be direct*, he surmised. No defenses, no excuses.

Most important—at the core of his whole plan—he accepted full responsibility: "I have sinned," he said. No blame-shifting. No excuses of hanging around the wrong crowd or having deep emotional wounds. "I have sinned . . . I am no longer worthy. . . ." Such a humble admission! Worthy once, but no longer, because of sin in his heart.

His plan was to volunteer for lowly service. "Make me as one of your hired men." He was willing to start at the bottom and stay there if necessary.

Finally, with his plan thought out, he acted. Maybe he washed his face in the pigs' water trough, shook the dust and heavy dirt from his robe, and started toward home.

Once he made his decision, his first steps were no doubt quick. Decisions motivate to action. But I wonder, with the pigpen in the distance and home a closer reality, if he didn't slow his steps. What would his father say? Would he be shocked? Should he have sent some kind of warning first? All kinds of doubts may have entered his mind as he got closer to home. But he knew his father. He would take his chances.

He had made the right choice. His father not only forgave

him but embraced him and welcomed him as a true son. And so the young man's dead-end obstacle gave way to a whole new beginning.

At times, I have been like this wayward son. I've gotten myself into some hard situations and found myself all alone, with no one to blame but myself.

I've had to retrace my steps and go back to ask for reconciliation. It's hard to do, but I've always been glad that I did. Now I can honestly thank God, who was waiting for me on the pathway home, for each obstacle that has brought me to my senses—and given me a chance for a new beginning.

---

What dead ends have you faced in your life?

What dead end threatens you right now?

Which would you prefer—seeing the dead end off in the distance and making the corrections necessary to avoid it, or finding yourself in a "pigpen" before you come to your senses? Why?

How can God use dead-end obstacles?

What new beginning do you need? Write a prayer, asking God for it.

# Blind Alleys—
# New
# Revelations

*"And we have the word of the prophets made more
certain, and you will do well to pay attention to it, as to
a light shining in a dark place, until the day dawns and
the morning star rises in your hearts."*

2 Peter 1:19

LET'S SAY your life is great. You are secure, serene, and at
peace. Then God whispers something into your spirit: There
is something you are convinced He wants you to do.

You swallow hard. What God seems to be asking may ruffle
things a bit. You like things smooth and calm, so you ignore
what you have heard in your heart and decide instead to com-
pensate for it by making sure your example—your righteousness, your untarnished witness—shows through. You convince
yourself that God didn't really mean for you to *do* what He
has shown you, but simply wants you to *pray about it.*

For the next little while life doesn't seem so bad. God, it
appears, has accepted your alternate plan. Then a storm starts
to brew in your spirit. God's Word is not as alive and exciting
anymore. Quiet times become a bore, then a chore. Uncer-
tainty replaces serenity, doubt corrodes peace.

Suddenly, it's evident you've turned into a blind alley.

There's no light, no direction, and no way out.

How do you turn a blind alley into new revelation?

God's Word tells us about another man who was instructed to do something for God—but didn't. Jonah was given specific instructions, where to go and what to say. Instead he caught a boat bound for another destination. Concerned about his reputation, he disregarded God's direction. Eventually, he found himself in the belly of a great fish.

Jonah's experience gives us the benefit of hope for getting out of the "blind alleys" we've entered.

1. *He recognized how he got into the mess.*

"This terrified [the sailors] and they asked, 'What have you done?' " (Jonah 1:10). They knew Jonah was running away from the Lord, because he'd already told them so.

2. *He took responsibility for his part and was ready to pay the consequences.*

" 'Pick me up and throw me into the sea,' he replied, 'and it will become calm. I know that it is my fault that this great storm has come upon you' " (Jonah 1:12).

3. *He surrendered.*

"Then they took Jonah and threw him overboard, and the raging sea grew calm" (Jonah 1:15).

4. *Then God moved on Jonah's behalf.*

But it wasn't at all what one would expect. A luxury schooner did not come along and rescue him, taking him to his original God-ordained destination. The end of Jonah's blind-alley experience was not yet.

God sent a great fish.

It was to get much darker before the light would shine again for Jonah.

5. *Jonah prayed.*

From inside the fish, at the end of the blind alley, Jonah cried out to God.

"He said: 'In my distress I called to the LORD, and he answered me. From the depths of the grave I called for help, and you listened to my cry' " (Jonah 2:2).

6. *It got worse before it got better.*

Jonah describes his experience like a terrifying amusement park ride.

"You hurled me into the deep, into the very heart of the seas, and the currents swirled about me; all your waves and breakers swept over me" (Jonah 2:3).

7. *Jonah attempted to bargain with God.*

Between gulps of seawater Jonah cried out to God and began to make all kinds of promises:

"I said, 'I have been banished from your sight; yet I will look again toward your holy temple' " (Jonah 2:4).

8. *He gave up hope.*

Plunged even deeper, he was convinced he would not survive:

"The engulfing waters threatened me, the deep surrounded me; seaweed was wrapped around my head. To the roots of the mountains I sank down; the earth beneath barred me in forever" (Jonah 2:5–6).

9. *He changed his focus.*

In the deepest, darkest part of his blind alley, he remembered God.

"But you brought my life up from the pit, O LORD my God. When my life was ebbing away, I remembered you, LORD, and my prayer rose to you, to your holy temple" (Jonah 2:6–7).

10. *He becomes thankful that he serves a living, powerful, wonderful God.*

"Those who cling to worthless idols forfeit the grace that would be theirs. But I, with a song of thanksgiving, will sacrifice to you. What I have vowed I will make good. Salvation comes from the LORD" (Jonah 2:8–9).

11. *God saved his life.*

Just when he is convinced God will save him—or maybe it's all a bad dream and he'll wake up in his own bed, or at least on his bunk in the boat—the environment begins closing in on him. The muscles of the great fish begin to contract and convulse.

"And the LORD commanded the fish, and it vomited Jonah onto dry land" (Jonah 2:10).

12. *Then God spoke again.*

"Then the word of the LORD came to Jonah a second time" (Jonah 3:1).

God speaks again. What a comforting thought. What God said once, He can say again.

"Go to the great city of Nineveh and proclaim to it the message I give you" (Jonah 3:2).

Do you think Jonah ignored God this time? Do you think he rang up his travel agent and booked another cruise?

"Jonah obeyed the word of the LORD and went to Nineveh" (Jonah 3:3).

I'm sure you'll agree that the three days it took to reach Nineveh were a joyous three days compared to those spent in the stomach of a fish. What God offers us in ways of service for Him might be a little difficult, but consider the options.

Haven't you prayed for God's will to be done *in* and *through* you? Don't believe for a moment that you have missed it. God hasn't changed His mind. Don't take chances with disobedience. The will of God calls you still. Obedience is not only the way out of your blind alley—it's a whale of a good deal!

---

What has God asked of you within the last year? The past month? The past week?

What have you said *no* to?

What "whale" is threatening to swallow you?

Have you attempted to bargain with God? How?

Would you like a second chance? Tell God about it in a written prayer.

# Chapter · 13 ·

## Stumbling Blocks— Stepping Stones

*"When Jesus spoke again to the people, he said, 'I am the light of the world. Whoever follows me will never walk in darkness, but will have the light of life.' "*

John 8:12

THERE WAS NO ONE like him ever before, nor would there be after. No one had ever shown the mighty power or performed the awesome deeds that he did. Now Moses was dead, and Joshua was called to take over. Before he died, Moses had laid hands on the young man and appointed him successor, anointed him with wisdom for leadership.

A nation of people with a land still to possess waited for Joshua's direction. They were camped within sight of the promised land, their promise actually in view.

God had given the promise, now He gave the command: "Prepare to take possession." He also reassured the people of His presence and provision.

But between the people and their promise stood a *problem*. Before them was a river too swift to swim. There was no ferry to carry them over, no bridge to cross.

They had good reason to doubt, wouldn't you say? Why struggle for the promise when the land on this side is almost as good as the land over there? We've come this far—can't we accept that our victory lies in how far we've come? Why do we have to go all the way?

"I'd settle for this. I like it here. I just got my tent-site all settled." Do any of these excuses sound familiar?

The children of promise could have let the river become a stumbling block instead of trusting God for stepping stones. They could have contented themselves with getting close, living within sight—and settled for less than God's best. Many of us do it all the time. Looking at obstacles, we let them become stumbling blocks when God intends that they become stepping stones.

How did the Israelites overcome their obstacle? How did the river become a walkway?

Appointed men took their places at each corner of the ark of the covenant, lifted it to their shoulders, and stepped tentatively into the water. As they did, the waters way upstream miraculously dammed themselves up. Standing midpoint in the riverbed, the waves waited until all the people made it safely across, then thundered down behind them.

Before the people reached the other side, twelve stones were lugged from the deepest part of the river bottom. When every last man, woman, and child were safely across, a memorial was built to remind future generations of how God made what could have been a stumbling block into stepping stones.

You too may be presented with a great difficulty before you inherit what God promises. You can let that problem be a stumbling block—if you choose.

Your problems can intimidate you. You can choose to live near the promise, within view of it. You may even be able to convince yourself that you're content. You can congratulate yourself on how far you've come and what it's taken you to get this far.

But nothing can keep you from reaching your promise unless you give up. No pain, no struggle, no past failure, no inability. *There is nothing that can prevent you from finding the strength to go on, unless you choose to camp on this side of God's promises.*

"For I am convinced that neither death nor life, neither

angels nor demons, neither the present nor the future, nor any powers, neither height nor depth, nor anything else in all creation, will be able to separate us from the love of God that is in Christ Jesus our Lord" (Romans 8:38–39).

————————

Can you let His love make the way for you to receive His promises?

What stumbling block do you want to see become a stepping stone?

What has God promised you?

What is in the way of your possessing that promise?

What would happen if God's presence entered that problem?

Chapter
· 14 ·

Obstacles—
Opportunities

*"We are hard pressed on every side, but not crushed;*
*perplexed, but not in despair; persecuted, but not*
*abandoned; struck down, but not destroyed. We always*
*carry around in our body the death of Jesus, so that the*
*life of Jesus may also be revealed in our body."*

2 Corinthians 4:8–10

IF YOU SINCERELY WANT to make sense of pain and struggle, it is required that you be able to see opportunity in obstacles. This is not the same as adopting a simplistic "silver-lining-in-every-cloud" philosophy. Rather, it means truly facing every obstacle, feeling every stress, and then, with determination, choosing to look beyond the obstacle to the opportunity you would not have otherwise.

Abraham's infertility gave him opportunity to receive word of a promised son and many descendants from three messengers. Esther was drafted into the harem of the king, and it gave her the opportunity to be an advocate for her people. Ruth saw beyond the obstacle of traveling to a foreign land with her mother-in-law, and it was the opportunity she needed to meet Boaz.

Who knows the obstacles Deborah faced as a woman in

71

an unusual position of authority as a judge of Israel before she was used in battle to win a mighty victory for God?

People today face obstacles, too. My friends, David and Karla, are examples of some who have.

David left a comfortable associate's position in a large church in Texas to pastor a small church split by factions and skilled in ruining the lives and ministries of its former pastors! David put his life and his reputation on the line and committed himself to shepherd a flock that seemed not only determined to abuse him but also to ruin him, if possible. Karla was committed to helping and supporting her husband.

In every crisis David saw an opportunity to break the church's patterns of self-destruction. When faced with rumor and slander, he saw it as an occasion to lead those men and women who had sinned against him to repentance and restoration. When persecuted and criticized, he fought the satanic strongholds that were entrenched in the lives of many of the members, rather than fight the members themselves.

When the people were ready to quit and close the doors to the church, David and Karla saw it as an opportunity for God to do something marvelous. When anonymous phone calls and threatening letters came, they suffered silently for the sake of Christ's name. When the few remaining faithful members became discouraged, my friends saw it as a chance to remain steady and unshakable. They found opportunities to love the people, slowly breaking down obstacles of rebellion and unloving attitudes. They even found a way to stay when everything and everyone told them to leave.

David faced obstacles of unbelief with faith. Karla witnessed to neighbors when the church members wouldn't listen to her husband's sermons. They accepted the people when faced with the obstacle of their rejection.

Knowing the truth of what had been done to the last pastor, David sought to reach out and restore him. Financial obstacles were opportunities to simplify, streamline, and manage differently. Broken equipment meant finding ways to do things without it.

David announced 6 A.M. prayer meetings on Wednesdays, and attended them alone. He fasted and prayed, believing God had given him a rare opportunity to develop his own character and spiritual stamina.

He and his wife were the only ones who showed up on church clean-up days. "It's an opportunity to do it our way," David once told me with a smile.

Every Sunday for weeks and months he reminded the congregation, "God's up to something." And the people would sit, arms crossed, wearing sour expressions, as if daring God to carry on. With his own unique perspective, this young shepherd saw an opportunity for God to surprise a few people.

He waited, and God did do something surprising.

A few people scattered—unfortunately to cause trouble in other churches. Then a few new people began to come, who didn't know how to be sour, rejecting, and abusive. They were people who wanted God to do something wonderful, and loved the pastor who believed that God would do just that.

This pastor came to a church filled with obstacles and saw a multitude of opportunities. The last time I talked with him, he confirmed that he wasn't the only one who saw opportunity—God did, too. God saw an opportunity to take a fractured church and make it whole. God saw an opportunity to build within this young man's life and heart a determined vision and love for God's work, and He did that.

Above all else, God has shown the life and love of Jesus to many through the lives of my friends, David and Karla.

---

In spite of all the obstacles you face, right now—at this very moment—God wants to show the life and love of Jesus through you, too. Will you let Him? Will you allow Him to turn your obstacles into opportunities?

What obstacle is threatening you right now?

Because of it, what opportunities do you have now that you wouldn't have otherwise?

What opportunity does God have to work in your life while helping you deal with this obstacle?

Are you making some decisions about obstacles and opportunities in your life?

Express your new decisions in a prayer.

# Chapter · 15 ·

## Betterness—Not Bitterness

*"My comfort in my suffering is this: Your promise preserves my life."*

Psalm 119:50

IF ANYONE EVER HAD a reason to be bitter it was Naomi. Far from home, her husband and both her sons had fallen ill and died. With no way to provide for herself, in grief, she turned to her daughters-in-law and begged them to return to their families. She had nothing to offer.

" 'Don't call me Naomi,' she told them. 'Call me Mara, because the Almighty has made my life very bitter. I went away full, but the LORD has brought me back empty. Why call me Naomi? The LORD has afflicted me; the Almighty has brought misfortune upon me' " (Ruth 1:20–21).

Hurt and discouraged, Naomi said goodbye to Orpah. Then she turned to Ruth. But Ruth would not leave her. She insisted on staying with Naomi, and together they traveled back to Judah.

Naomi found her strength to go on, *together* with Ruth. She didn't keep the name Mara, because her life did not remain bitter. Naomi loved Ruth, and together they built a new life. Later there was a new husband, then a new baby. Naomi chose *betterness* instead of *bitterness*.

Is an obstacle of bitterness keeping you from a new life? You too can choose betterness. Living our lives, solving our problems, facing our obstacles according to God's Word guarantees sweetness, joy, and hope.

When tempted to be bitter, remember these six important principles:

1. *God knows what you are going through.*

"The LORD said, 'I have indeed seen the misery of my people in Egypt. I have heard them crying out because of their slave drivers, and I am concerned about their suffering' " (Exodus 3:7).

2. *He feels what you feel.*

"In all their distress he too was distressed, and the angel of his presence saved them. In his love and mercy he redeemed them; he lifted them up and carried them all the days of old" (Isaiah 63:9).

"Therefore, since we have a great high priest who has gone through the heavens, Jesus the Son of God, let us hold firmly to the faith we profess. For we do not have a high priest who is unable to sympathize with our weaknesses, but we have one who has been tempted in every way, just as we are—yet was without sin" (Hebrews 4:14–15).

3. *He is on your side.*

"What, then, shall we say in response to this? If God is for us, who can be against us? He who did not spare his own Son, but gave him up for us all—how will he not also, along with him, graciously give us all things?" (Romans 8:31–32).

4. *He will work it out while He is at work in you.*

"And we know that in all things God works for the good of those who love him, who have been called according to his purpose" (Romans 8:28).

5. *You can be encouraged—hope is ahead.*

"So we fix our eyes not on what is seen, but on what is unseen. For what is seen is temporary, but what is unseen is eternal" (2 Corinthians 4:18).

Writer and speaker Jack Taylor says this: "Trouble is bound to come. But trouble is also bound to go, and joy is bound to follow."

You may have been drinking from waters of bitterness, but today Jesus is offering you a fresh cool drink from the sweet waters of *betterness*.

"Whoever drinks the water I give him will never thirst. Indeed, the water I give him will become in him a spring of water welling up to eternal life" (John 4:14).

———————

What bitter experiences have you been through?

In what ways have you carried bitterness?

If you weren't carrying bitterness, how would your life change?

If you have been struggling with obstacles of bitterness and want betterness instead, tell the Lord that in prayer.

Which obstacles have you chosen to overcome:
Dead ends
Blind alleys
Stumbling blocks
Circumstantial obstacles
Bitterness

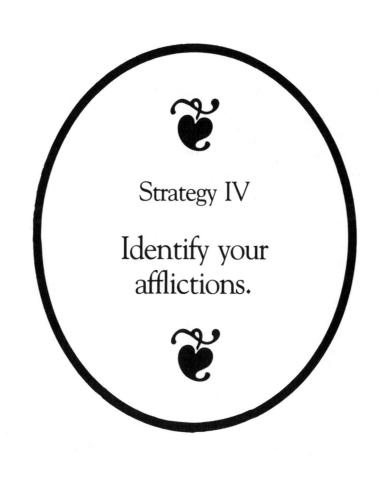

Strategy IV

Identify your
afflictions.

*F*or our struggle is not against flesh and blood, but against the rulers, against the authorities, against the powers of this dark world and against the spiritual forces of evil in the heavenly realms.

EPHESIANS 6:12

TO MOST OF US, afflictions are physical limitations or pain. The Bible gives us many examples of physical afflictions; its pages are filled with tender scenes of Christ's compassion as He touched those afflicted with physical pain.

There was the woman with the issue of blood. For twelve years she was miserable and hopeless, but she would not give up. One day, Jesus came by; she was able to reach out and touch Him, and was instantly and wonderfully healed. All four Gospel accounts—Matthew, Mark, Luke, and John— shine with miraculous moments when Jesus touched and healed those afflicted with physical problems. Leprosy, paralysis, blindness, deafness, crippled limbs, and many other afflictions fled at the touch of the Master Healer. The Bible also tells of others who were afflicted with the consequences of their own sinful actions. There are stories of mothers crippled by ambition, and of kings afflicted by lust and power.

Affliction comes in many forms. Many people, if you were to ask them, would not consider themselves afflicted because they don't suffer with health problems. Sadly, they continue with their inner pain, when their lives could be in full bloom and producing sweet fruit. Pain becomes a way of life, and hope dies.

This strategy is designed to bring *sense* to your afflictions. It will help you identify them and make a difference in how you order your life because of them. In this section we will identify five afflictions many suffer today, and look into God's Word for our encouragement. We will consider the following: assault by the devil; pounding circumstances; suffering the results of taking things into our own hands; never being able to measure up; and too-heavy responsibilities.

# Chapter · 16 ·

# Assaulted by the Devil

*"Jesus traveled about from one town and village to another, proclaiming the good news of the kingdom of God. The Twelve were with him, and also some women who had been cured of evil spirits and diseases: Mary (called Magdalene) from whom seven demons had come out; Joanna the wife of Cuza, the manager of Herod's household; Susanna; and many others. These women were helping to support them out of their own means."*

(Luke 8:1–3)

## "THE MAGDALENE MALADY"

Meet Mary—outgoing in public, miserable in private. She was a woman of influence, a woman of position and means, and yet she was troubled by assaults of the Devil. Something much stronger had control of her. Mary was demon-possessed. Seven demons had attacked and invaded her, then drove her without mercy, so that she lived in a personal hell. Then she met Jesus—and her whole life changed. Mary the tormented became Mary the triumphant.

We need not attribute every cross moment, every sinful or compulsive action to Satan or to demons—though as Christians we do believe there are dark influences around us. But perhaps you, too, enjoy good standing in your church or community while living each day in your own personal hell. Are destructive habits, negative attitudes, and harassing fears your constant companions? Do you push politeness to the extreme, hoping no one will guess how you resent their intrusion into your personal space? Are you the type who says yes to every request, then desperately looks for ways to back out of the commitment?

Maybe you have personal habits or impure thoughts that keep you bound and shamed. Or perhaps you suffer from an addiction that controls your life.

I have wonderful news. The same Jesus who freed Mary can free you. She was delivered from her malady and you can be, too.

The freedom Christ offers turns victims into victors. Those who once fell under the assault of the Devil can now take hold of the full authority that comes to us in Jesus' name. Persecution gives way to praise, and warfare ends in worship.

You no longer have to be known by the battles you fight, but by the victories you win.

No longer afflicted with the "Magdalene Malady"—like Mary, you have become a *Magdalene Miracle*!

---

In what ways are you most likely to be assaulted by evil influences?

If Satan were to try to intimidate you, what relationships would he most likely use?

What fear is most likely to threaten your peace?

What single failure is most likely to torment you?

How has Christ touched your life? What difference has that made?

What power does the enemy *claim* to have over you?

What power does the enemy *actually* have over you?

What do the promises of the following verses from Psalm 34 mean to you:

"Those who look to [God] are radiant; their faces are never covered with shame."

"This poor man called, and the LORD heard him; he saved him out of all his troubles."

"The angel of the LORD encamps around those who fear him, and he delivers them."

"Taste and see that the LORD is good; blessed is the man who takes refuge in him."

"Fear the LORD, you his saints, for those who fear him lack nothing."

# Chapter · 17 ·

## Overwhelmed By Circumstances

" 'Don't call me Naomi,' she told them. 'Call me Mara,
because the Almighty has made my life very bitter. I went
away full, but the LORD has brought me back empty . . .
The LORD has afflicted me; the Almighty has brought
misfortune upon me.' "

(Ruth 1:20–21)

## "THE MARA MISERY"

Naomi was all alone, far from home, and feelin' blue—the
stuff of which country songs are written. Her life was quite a
change from ten years before, when she and her husband took
their two sons and set out for Moab and the chance for a better
life!

For ten years the dream was working. Naomi saw her two
strong sons grow up and marry Moabite women. Then tragedy
struck, and her whole life crumbled. Her husband died, *and*
her two sons. Without them she had no support. She had her
two daughters-in-law, but no way to provide for them. Life's
hard knocks overwhelmed her and Naomi lost her taste for
living. "Call me Mara . . ." she said. "Call me *bitter*."

When Naomi's circumstances became more than she could
handle alone, she wanted family—she wanted to go home.

Naturally, many of us turn toward home when we are overwhelmed by trouble. Here she was—husbandless, childless, penniless, and setting out alone on a difficult journey over rough terrain. Or so she thought. But Naomi was more blessed than she realized: She had Ruth.

Ruth was not about to abandon her mother-in-law. She joined herself to Naomi, not only for the duration of the journey but for life. Ruth, once her daughter-in-law, now became her best friend and her best *hope*. For it was through Ruth that Naomi's life changed again.

Returning as she did to the land of Israel, Naomi was considered a beggar, in need of someone to redeem her from a forgotten existence of poverty. And it was because of Ruth that Naomi met a man named Boaz—a kinsman, and the "redeemer" she needed.

Through Boaz's marriage to Ruth, Naomi regained her joy. Ruth became the connection, and Obed was the result. Naomi's lap became a grandma's lap after all. Naomi's "Mara Misery" gave way to a "Boaz Breakthrough."

Whatever circumstance threatens you, whatever bitter experience intimidates you, remember this: You too have a Kinsman Redeemer. His name is Jesus. According to law, Boaz had to pay a price in order to marry Ruth. Jesus has already paid that price for you. Boaz had to go through proper legal channels for Ruth, just as Jesus intercedes before the Father for you.

Like Naomi, a "Boaz Breakthrough" is waiting for you. Call upon Jesus' precious, blessed name, and circumstances that have tormented you will begin to change. Bitter experiences that harass you will become sweetness as He touches them with His mercy. The pain that has dominated your life and affected your decisions must subside when embraced by His comfort and love.

Let Jesus redeem not only *you*, but the hard places of your life. Accept your own personal "Boaz Breakthrough."

What circumstances are crushing your joy?

What bitterness is jeopardizing your peace?

What is alarming you?

Ruth led Naomi to Boaz. Who has lead you to Christ? Identify the "Ruths" in your life.

Who is your Kinsman Redeemer?

Write about your own "Boaz Breakthrough."

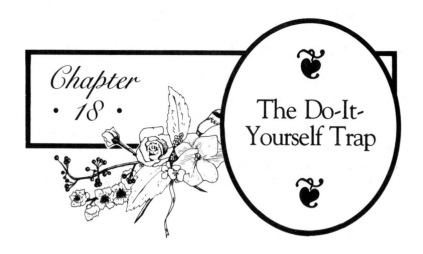

# Chapter · 18 ·

# The Do-It-Yourself Trap

*"So she said to Abram, 'The LORD has kept me from having children. Go, sleep with my maidservant; perhaps I can build a family through her.' Abram agreed to what Sarai said. So after Abram had been living in Canaan ten years, Sarai his wife took her Egyptian maidservant Hagar and gave her to her husband to be his wife."*

Genesis 16:2

## "THE SARAH SYNDROME"

Sarah loved Abraham. Her marriage was built not only on love, but on respect and partnership. Where he went she went—not as a shadow, but as a strong influence. By his love and respect for her, we can see that Sarah enjoyed an equality with Abraham that was rare for a woman in her day.

Abraham's dreams were her dreams. She shared his dangers and felt his heartaches; she took whatever risks were necessary to make him happy and to protect his interests.

She lived through adversity as well as prosperity. She shared responsibility and took authority in her husband's absence.

Further, Sarah remained loyal to Abraham, even when he lied about their relationship and allowed Egyptians to carry her off. She was a woman of great strength and depth of character.

But like so many capable women, she developed a set of symptoms that, when left unchecked, only lead to trouble. Her life became marred by what we might call the "Sarah Syndrome"—that is, taking things into our own hands. When we do so, we will find ourselves living with the sour consequences of a do-it-yourself life.

The "Sarah Syndrome" is marked by specific symptoms:

1. *Impatience.*

Sarah became impatient waiting for God's promise to be fulfilled.

2. *No understanding of divine delay.*

She did not understand that if God could give her a baby at seventy-five, He could give her one at ninety. She did not understand that God, the Promise-Giver, would alone be responsible for the timing of the promise.

3. *Jumping to the wrong conclusions.*

She concluded, as so many do, that she was the problem or the obstacle—It is my fault; I am standing in the way; I am supposed to do something—to humble myself and step aside, or to offer an alternate plan.

4. *Devising an alternative plan to "help" the promise along.*

The hope for the baby of promise gave way to the reality of the baby of her own "great" idea.

5. *No satisfaction.*

With a life marred by a plan that backfired, Sarah ended up with a giant *Hagar Hassle.* How sad to finally realize that the alternative is not the solution—and that there is no way to turn back the situation we have created! Sarah could not erase Ishmael—or Hagar's disrespectful attitude—and now she had a baby, but she did not have the promise.

6. *Complaining.*

Oh, woe is me! This is miserable. I can't take it anymore. What shall I do now? A life full of groaning and moaning is often a symptom of the "Sarah Syndrome."

7. *Shifting the blame.*

Abraham was willing—maybe too willing. Hagar didn't hesitate, either. *The idea was a good one,* Sarah might have thought, *but you two have messed it all up. It's not my fault that the idea didn't work!* (See Genesis 16:5.)

8. *Making the best of a bad situation.*

Moans of complaint become sighs of resignation. *This is the way it is; this is the way it will be. Oh, well—we'll just live with it. We'll survive it somehow.*

But this is where the story takes a turn for the better. The final outcome of Sarah's life is not that of one who learned to live unhappily-ever-after. Though her life was one continuous trial of her faith in God's promise that she was to be the Mother of Nations, she emerged as a woman of power. She was a dutiful and beloved wife. And she did become a favored and adored mother eventually.

How did Sarah finally overcome her do-it-yourself syndrome and realize God's promise? What made the difference? Sarah found a way to change. What was her solution?

1. *She heard a word from the Lord.*

"Then the LORD said, 'I will surely return to you about this time next year, and Sarah your wife will have a son.' Now Sarah was listening at the entrance to the tent, which was behind him" (Genesis 18:10).

2. *She submitted to God.*

3. *She realized God moves in His time, on His terms, in His way, for His purposes.*

"Now the LORD was gracious to Sarah as he had said, and the LORD did for Sarah what he had promised. Sarah became pregnant and bore a son to Abraham in his old age, at the very time God had promised him" (Genesis 21:1–2).

4. *She used wisdom in dealing with unbearable situations.*

"The child grew and was weaned, and on the day Isaac was weaned Abraham held a great feast. But Sarah saw that the son whom Hagar the Egyptian had borne to Abraham was mocking, . . . (Genesis 21:8–9).

5. *She asked for justice.*

" . . . And she said to Abraham, 'Get rid of that slave woman and her son, for that slave woman's son will never share in the inheritance with my son Isaac' " (Genesis 21:10).

6. *She experienced freedom.*

"Early the next morning Abraham took some food and a skin of water and gave them to Hagar. He set them on her shoulders and then sent her off with the boy. She went on her way and wandered in the desert of Beersheba" (Genesis 21:14).

The lessons to be learned from Sarah are appropriate for today. Women of strength and capability often are afflicted by the "Sarah Syndrome." But there is hope—the same six steps Sarah took are today's remedy as well. Come on, do-it-yourselfers, let go, and let God do it! Why settle for a "Hagar Hassle" when you can have the *promise*?

———

Are you a do-it-yourselfer?

Name one time when you took things into your own hands and ended up with sour consequences.

Identify a situation when you waited for God to work it out

according to His time and purpose.

What are you waiting for now?

How will the "Sarah Syndrome" analogy help you to wait?

Which is the affliction—waiting, or living with the consequences of being a do-it-yourselfer? Why?

## Chapter · 19 ·

# Never Good Enough

*"And Jacob . . . finished the week with Leah, and then
Laban gave him his daughter Rachel to be his wife.
Jacob lay with Rachel also, and he loved Rachel
more than Leah."*

Genesis 29:28, 30

## "THE LEAH LEGACY"

Imagine Leah's sadness. She always lived in the shadow of
her lovely and charming sister, Rachel. She was known as
"the plain one" compared to "the pretty one," "the dull one"
next to "the smart and witty one." It's hard to be the unfavored
child. And it's doubly hard when the culture demands that
the eldest sister marry first—even though the younger sister is
more desirable.

Can you even begin to identify with the pain of knowing
the man you are marrying thinks he is marrying your sister?
Can you conceive of a wedding night in which you know all
along that your handsome groom thinks you are someone else?

Leah fights to stifle her tears as Jacob lifts the wedding veil.
His look of disappointment explodes into rage. His anger con-
firms that she is not his choice.

"Laban!" Jacob throws the flap of the tent open. "You

deceived me! You tricked me with Leah. Where is my promised Rachel?"

Unloved, unappreciated, unwanted—will this be Leah's only destiny? Is she doomed to this painful existence all her life?

There are women who feel like Leah, who live her legacy every day—women who are abused, used, and passed off to another as a piece of property. Others live "Leah's Legacy" to a lesser degree. Some are trapped into marriage, perhaps by an unwanted pregnancy, or by pressure from a parent, or by the fear that no one else will ever come along. Some live as "substitutes," knowing that if someone better does come along, their positions, their jobs, or their marriages are history.

For those afflicted with the "Leah Legacy," there is hope. Leah may have been unloved and unappreciated by her family and then by her husband, but not by God. God loved her, cared for her, and gave her a special advantage. She could give Jacob something that even the charming, desirable Rachel could not—Leah could bear children. God can give you a special advantage, too—the advantage of knowing Him.

God's promises are precious to those who are in pain and who feel the rejection of being the "second choice." His promises offer life and hope to those who never seem to measure up or to win the blue ribbon.

If you are afflicted with the "Leah Legacy," there are several important things God wants you to know:

1. *He remembers you and does not ignore your needs.*

"For he who avenges blood remembers; he does not ignore the cry of the afflicted" (Psalm 9:12).

"But Zion said, 'The LORD has forsaken me, the Lord has forgotten me. Can a mother forget the baby at her breast and have no compassion on the child she has borne? Though she may forget, I will not forget you!' " (Isaiah 49:14–15).

2. *Only He can and will supply all your needs.*

"The LORD will guide you always; he will satisfy your needs in a sun-scorched land and will strengthen your frame. You will be like a well-watered garden, like a spring whose waters never fail" (Isaiah 58:11).

"And my God will meet all your needs according to his glorious riches in Christ Jesus" (Philippians 4:19).

3. *He gives strength to you just when you need it.*

"The LORD gives strength to his people; the LORD blesses his people with peace" (Psalm 29:11).

4. *He promises to wipe away all your tears.*

"He will wipe every tear from their eyes. There will be no more death or mourning or crying or pain, for the old order of things has passed away" (Revelation 21:4).

Rachel was loved more by Jacob. But Leah was not less loved by God. While Rachel was favored by a man, Leah was blessed by the Maker of the Universe.

If you are afflicted with the "Leah Legacy," reach out for her blessing. Lean on God, not on any person, for your love and acceptance. God does not accept you because He has no choice—He accepts you because He loves you.

————

How have you experienced the "Leah Legacy"?

What is to be your main source of strength and comfort?

Who loved you enough to die for you?




Who will never abuse you or cause you harm?




Express your love to Him in your own words.

## Chapter · 20 ·

## Too-Heavy Responsibilities

*"A Canaanite woman from that vicinity came to him, crying out, 'Lord, Son of David, have mercy on me! My daughter is suffering terribly . . .' "*

Matthew 15:22

HAVE MERCY ON ME? What is this woman saying? Her daughter is suffering terribly, yet she asks for mercy for herself. How can that be?

Many years ago I knew a young wife and mother I'll call Arlene. Her young daughter, Crissy, began to have seizures and was taken to the doctor. In the days and months that followed she spent long, endless hours in university hospital clinics and specialists' offices. She saw her beloved child subjected to many painful and inconclusive medical tests.

Arlene's church was called to fast and pray for Crissy's healing. The members rallied around Arlene and her family and trusted God for a miracle. But when Crissy became worse, they began to ask personal and insensitive questions of Arlene and her husband. Some suggested that Arlene and her husband didn't have enough faith, or that they somehow had caused Crissy's condition. Well-meaning Christians began to suggest all kinds of reasons for the problem and to offer all sorts of odd remedies. Soon Arlene grew weary, not only because of Crissy's health problems, but because of the Christians whom she needed for encouragement and support.

One Sunday after an evening worship service, Arlene walked up to the front of the church for prayer. "I can't take it anymore," she cried. "I'm tired. I don't know what to do for Crissy, and I don't know how to answer all the questions." She knelt in the front of the church, looking thin and distressed.

"We've taken Crissy for prayer ministry—we even took her for prayers of deliverance. We've been to every medical specialist. We control everything she eats, and she takes all the drugs that have been prescribed for her. We have done everything we've been told to do. But you can see for yourself, she isn't better, she only gets worse.

"I have to drive her to school every day, and be available by phone in case she has a seizure that they can't handle," she told us that night. "I have to pick her up from school because she can't ride the bus anymore. I can't take her shopping with me, and I can't let her stay at her grandma's house overnight. I have to be available twenty-four hours a day—" She gripped my hands as she sobbed. "It looks like I'll have to live like this for the rest of Crissy's life."

Arlene felt alone. She saw no end to her challenge. She wondered if she would have the strength to make it through the days, weeks, months, and years to come.

The Canaanite woman in Matthew 15 prayed Arlene's heartfelt prayer, "Lord, have mercy on *me*."

Caregivers need mercy. They walk the fine line between caregiving and caretaking. They try to adjust to living under permanent stress without giving up hope for healing and change. They face terrible reality every day, and they consciously, purposely fight to maintain a level of faith in order to survive.

It would be so easy to give in to depression and self-pity in a situation like Arlene's. It is tempting to be angry at God when He doesn't seem to answer; to be disgusted with Christians who seem to have all the answers.

101

The only thing I could say to Arlene that night as we prayed was this: "I don't know why God doesn't heal Crissy. I don't know why all our prayers concerning her aren't answered. But this I do know—God knows how you hurt, and He cares. I don't know why Crissy isn't being healed, but I do know God heals. I don't know why she isn't better, but I know He has heard our prayers."

For the first time since Crissy became ill, Arlene and I prayed together. It was not a prayer for Crissy, but for Arlene.

Arlene prayed for mercy, not for Crissy, but for herself. Was she being selfish? I don't think so. God has given her a special assignment—a special trust. He has not sent answers, but He has sent His love and His strength.

Crissy is approaching twenty years of age now, and her seizures have not abated. She is smaller than other women her age, and the seizures have crippled her mind. Still she smiles and talks about how she loves Jesus and her mother.

What has made the difference for Arlene all these years? "I asked for mercy," she explains simply, "and God gave me grace. Sometimes I ask God to show me His presence, and Crissy gives me one of her smiles and tells me she loves me. It hasn't been easy," she admits, "but I have had Crissy."

Are you a caregiver? Have you sought answers and healing for someone in your care with no results? Perhaps you are one of a growing number of people sandwiched between elderly parents and the needs of your children. Are you pressured by the pain of someone near to you? If so, it's perfectly appropriate to pray for yourself and ask for mercy. The Canaanite woman needed it, Arlene needed it, and you need it.

If you are living with a caregiver's challenge, you need all the courage you can get. Ask God for His mercy, not only for the one you are caring for, but for *yourself*. Ask for His mercy, and expect His grace.

---

When you are giving care to another and you get tired, why

are you tempted to feel guilty?

What do you do when you see someone who desperately needs a healing touch from God and He doesn't seem to answer?

How do you treat someone who has been afflicted for a long time?

Do you know a caregiver who could use a friend? Could you be that friend?

You may not have recognized your own particular affliction in any of those covered in this section. If that is the case, how would you describe your own long-lasting pain or trouble?

What theme runs through all the afflictions written about in this section, and how can you apply it to your situation?

Strategy V

Know who you
are in Christ.

*F*or we are God's workmanship, created in Christ Jesus to do good works, which God prepared in advance for us to do.

EPHESIANS 2:10

AFTER FOURTEEN YEARS on death row, Robert Alton Harris died in California's gas chamber. Every conceivable appeal had been made in his behalf, and each one was denied. There was never any doubt about his guilt, but questions were raised about his emotional and mental condition at the time of his crimes. At the very end, his death sentence was challenged, not on the question of *innocence*, but on the question of *responsibility*.

Jesus was also tried, convicted, and sentenced to death. The difference between these two stories is a study in contrasts and opposites.

Harris was known to be guilty; Jesus was known to be innocent. Harris was judged to be responsible for crimes he *did* commit; while Jesus was held responsible for crimes he *did not* commit.

The life and death of the criminal seem tragic and senseless; but the life and death of Jesus were full of purpose, and resulted in the miracle of His resurrection.

Jesus, the innocent Son of God, was placed in the hands of a merciless and illegal court. He hung on the cross and died a torturous death. It is said that He was born to die. He died for you and for me so that we could live victoriously over sin and over our circumstances while living in relationship with God our Father.

It was not Jesus' sin and guilt that took Him to the cross, but ours. He took upon himself our shame, our shortcomings, and our afflictions. And He rose again to share His resurrection life with us. As He abides in us, and we abide in Him, we become different people—people who make a difference. We are changed—we are transformed.

The cross is not a status symbol. It is a symbol of hope, of life, and of change.

Because of Jesus, we can live a changed life every day: relationally, spiritually, legally, culturally, and eternally. To know Jesus is to invite change. As we explore the changes open to us, we can come to know who we are in Christ. And that makes all the difference.

# Chapter · 21 ·

## Bought at a Price

*"You are not your own; you were bought at a price."*
1 Corinthians 6:19–20

SIX MONTHS AFTER we brought our daughter home, we went to court and sat before a very important-looking judge. He listened to our lawyer, keeping one eye on him and one eye on the paperwork scattered across his desk. Eventually the lawyer finished and the judge looked at the baby in my arms. Then he looked over the top of his glasses at me and finally at my husband. He cleared his throat, held his gavel above a small wooden block and paused. Only the small twinkle in his eye betrayed his serious demeanor. Smacking the gavel down, he said, "Granted." Standing, he extended his hand to my husband. "Congratulations! You're a good-looking family," he said. "Let's see you in here next year with your second one."

Our little Rhonda *legally* became our daughter that day. Leaving the judge's chambers, I stepped into the hall a full-fledged, legal mother. I held my baby close to me and sobbed into her blanket. For six months we had been her custodians, but now we were her parents! Before, she had access to everything we had, but now she had title to it. Through adoption she became our heir. It wasn't the very next year, but soon we appeared again with our second daughter, Sandra, in our arms. With Rhonda in tow, we repeated the process, so that Sandra became a joint heir with her older sister.

You, too, have become an heir. Jesus has come before God and all the universe to present you for adoption into His family. By accepting His redemptive work, your legal status has changed: You have become an heir!

"For he chose us in him before the creation of the world to be holy and blameless in his sight. In love he predestined us to be adopted as his sons through Jesus Christ, in accordance with his pleasure and will—to the praise of his glorious grace, which he has freely given us in the One he loves" (Ephesians 1:4–6).

"If you belong to Christ, then you are Abraham's seed, and heirs according to the promise" (Galatians 3:29).

"Now if we are children, then we are heirs—heirs of God and co-heirs with Christ, if indeed we share in his sufferings in order that we may also share in his glory" (Romans 8:17).

"So you are no longer a slave, but a son; and since you are a son, God has made you also an heir" (Galatians 4:7).

You were granted a changed status, both legally and spiritually, when you accepted Jesus Christ. As His heir, you now share all rights, privileges, and responsibilities with Jesus. You also bear some responsibility in fulfilling His purpose, and you are entrusted with stewardship over everything He places into your hands. As an heir, you can understand more about His purpose, and you can grow in a more complete understanding of His will.

When we adopted our daughters, our relationship with them (while sealed by the state of Minnesota and signed by a judge) was really only beginning. It was up to us to instill our values in our children, teach them obedience and loving discipline, and lead them to a knowledge of Jesus Christ so that they might accept Him as their Savior.

So it is when we accept Jesus. Our relationship has only begun. As God's children we are expected to learn our position of authority in the "family business"—which is the kingdom of God. All the legal requirements have been met; now the training begins.

Once sinners, we are now children of God. Once bound,

110

we are now free. Once abandoned, we are now adopted. Once abused, we are now loved. Once doomed to die, we are now destined to live. We are His people. We have every reason to praise God; we have every legal right to come before Him, to embrace Him, to reach into His heart. We are His children— and He loves us.

---

When we adopted our girls, they were given our name. What name have you been given to use?

How does knowing your change in legal status help you to know who you are in Christ?

Finish this statement: Legally, in Christ I am. . . .

# Chapter · 22 ·

## "Papa, God"

*"For you did not receive a spirit that makes you a slave
again to fear, but you received the Spirit of sonship. And
by him we cry, 'Abba, Father.' "*

Romans 8:15

AFTER PRESIDENT John F. Kennedy was assassinated, his family, friends, and staff went into mourning. A nation and a world tried to make some sense out of the pain. Those closest to the President had to somehow go on with their lives. Some of the staff had to find other jobs, resume their own lives, and set new goals.

President Kennedy's children, who were very young at the time of his death, built a memorial library, when they were grown, in honor of their father. Recently, Caroline and John Kennedy, Jr. were interviewed and shared some of the pictures from the library. One especially tugged at my heart: John, Jr. was playing under the presidential desk, right at the President's feet; President Kennedy wasn't president to John, Jr.—he was Daddy. A major magazine once ran a picture of President John Kennedy rocking John, Jr. on his lap while holding a conference with an important head of state.

I think of myself as having that kind of access to God. I

can approach Him at any time. Even during His normal working day, when He is busy with the affairs of kingdoms and nations I can come close to Him, just to be near Him. I don't always have to have a request or important agenda—I can come just because I like to be with Him. You see, for me, God isn't only the Creator of the Universe—He's my Papa.

When you and I received Jesus, we became His children: "To all who received him, to those who believed in his name, he gave the right to become children of God—children born not of natural descent, nor of human decision or a husband's will, but born of God" (John 1:12–13).

And furthermore, we were given the key to the door of His office.

"Let us then approach the throne of grace with confidence" (Hebrews 4:16).

"In him and through faith in him we may approach God with freedom and confidence" (Ephesians 3:12).

When we entered a relationship with God through Jesus, we obtained our "security clearance." We were given a new identity: " 'I will be a Father to you, and you will be my sons and daughters,' says the Lord Almighty" (2 Corinthians 6:18).

I once lived apart from God, doomed to isolation and loneliness. But because of Jesus that has all changed. Now I am a child of God, part of His family, and I live in relationship with Him. Knowing who I am in Christ means that I must fully realize my relationship with my "Papa, God"; take advantage of the privilege of knowing Him; and find every excuse and reason for entering His presence as often as I can.

---

What keeps you from entering God's "office" and "playing under His desk"?

If you were to climb up on God's lap and He were to tell you the story of how He loved you and found you, how would He begin?




If God were to reach into His pocket and take out a special treasure for you, what do you think it would be?




How does being secure in God's love and your relationship with Him make coping with your present struggles easier?

# Chapter · 23 ·

## Life in a New Dimension

*"And if the Spirit of him who raised Jesus from the dead is living in you, he who raised Christ from the dead will also give life to your mortal bodies through his Spirit, who lives in you."*

Romans 8:11

IT CAME YESTERDAY just as I was eating lunch—*bad news.* Dumbfounded, shaken by the crisis now flung in my face, I stared at my food, unable to eat.

But soon this particular crisis will be over, and I'll be back on my feet once again. How can I be so sure? Because I've received bad news and faced crises before.

I watched our family home burn to the ground when I was about ten years old. A couple of years later, my sister was badly injured in an automobile accident. My grandfather's death came suddenly when I was thirteen, and my parents separated during my last year in junior high school.

Later as an adult, I stood by helplessly as my three-year-old underwent eye surgery. I miscarried and lost a long-prayed-for baby. My grandmother's death was difficult for me because we were such good friends, and that loss was shortly followed by an accident in which my teenage daughter broke her neck.

Then my father became ill one Easter Sunday, and died within three months—just two weeks after my oldest daughter's wedding. There have been other crises as well: financial, marital—you name it.

But let me tell you something wonderful: I know the faithfulness of God's Spirit within me! His Spirit strengthens me, comforts, guides, and protects me.

People all around me live with many of the same or similar crises. Maybe you are facing a particularly challenging time right now.

How do we navigate such stressful times? I suggest that we begin by taking hold of several important truths:

1. *God's life within us does not exempt us from the realities of this life, but adds a new dimension to it, as we saw in Romans 8:11.*

2. *God's life within us does not mean we will not feel pain, but that we will have the strength to endure it and grow through it.*

"When you pass through the waters, I will be with you; and when you pass through the rivers, they will not sweep over you. When you walk through the fire, you will not be burned; the flames will not set you ablaze" (Isaiah 43:2).

3. *We face crises head-on, knowing that we can do whatever the situation requires—all the while aware that beyond the practical matter lies a spiritual dimension.*

"For our struggle is not against flesh and blood, but against the rulers, against the authorities, against the powers of this dark world and against the spiritual forces of evil in the heavenly realms" (Ephesians 6:12).

4. *We find the strength to carry on our regular duties and go about our daily lives, and the ability to maintain our hope and joy from God's Spirit stirring within us. Whenever situations would drain the very life from us, we must remember we have a new Life-source—God himself.*

"For it is God who works in you to will and to act according to his good purpose" (Philippians 2:13).

5. *Because of Jesus we don't live under the circumstances—we can live above them.*

"Who shall separate us from the love of Christ? Shall trouble or hardship or persecution or famine or nakedness or danger or sword? As it is written: 'For your sake we face death all day long; we are considered as sheep to be slaughtered.' No, in all these things we are more than conquerors through him who loved us" (Romans 8:35–37).

6. *By Him we find peace and joy.*

"Peace I leave with you; my peace I give you. I do not give to you as the world gives. Do not let your hearts be troubled and do not be afraid" (John 14:27).

7. *In our Lord and Savior we find our identity when our reputation is damaged.*

"How great is the love the Father has lavished on us, that we should be called children of God! And that is what we are! The reason the world does not know us is that it did not know him" (1 John 3:1).

8. *Through Him we go to God when we need someone to talk to openly and without reservation.*

"For through him we . . . have access to the Father by one Spirit" (Ephesians 2:18).

"In him and through faith in him we may approach God with freedom and confidence" (Ephesians 3:12).

9. *With Jesus by our side we answer our accusers.*

"The Lord is at your right hand . . ." (Psalm 110:5).

10. *Because of Jesus we are able to make sense of pain and struggle. Because of Him we have the strength to go on.*

"For he will command his angels concerning you to guard you in all your ways; they will lift you up in their hands, so that you will not strike your foot against a stone" (Psalm 91:11–12).

This is what it is like to be a child of God. This is living life in a new dimension. Not that we don't make mistakes. Not that we are exempt from pain and confusion and struggle—but we are given unshakable strength. Strength to endure, strength to persevere—strength to win!

Living life in the new dimension means that we are no longer afraid to feel the pain of our struggles, and that we are confident of the strength to go on.

––––––––––

If we are no longer afraid, and we have confidence we will have the strength to carry on, why do you think we fight to deny the painful things that have happened to us?

Recall an event that you know you survived "because of Jesus."

What difference does life in a new dimension make in coping with everyday struggles?

What difference does living in a new dimension make in facing crises?

What difference does the new dimension make in evaluating problems and making decisions?

What difference does the new dimension make in facing accusations?

What difference does this make for you today?

# Chapter · 24 ·

# Being Different

*"Do not conform any longer to the pattern of this world, but be transformed by the renewing of your mind. Then you will be able to test and approve what God's will is— his good, pleasing and perfect will."*

Romans 12:2

"DON'T GET MAD—GET EVEN," says the world system. "Grab all you can get; and do unto others *before* they can do it to you." "Take things into your own hands; watch your back; don't trust anyone."

The world system also says, "Whatever feels good—do it!" It says if a pregnancy is inconvenient or may produce a less-than-perfect baby—get rid of it. It says that if two adults are in love they owe it to themselves to explore the deepest level of human communication, sexual pleasure, without the commitment of marriage. The world says that if a marriage is in trouble or difficult—bail out. It says that if your spouse or your friends are not meeting all your needs, get new ones.

The Christian culture is different. We don't conform to the world's patterns and standards. We order our lives and live them by the principles of God's Word.

We answer our accusers with truth, not anger. We choose

to live open-handedly and generously. We choose to make lifelong commitments and to love those in our lives with unconditional love. We make decisions to trust, even though we may have had our trust violated. We select attitudes based on what Jesus teaches instead of what life hands us. This is not a legalistic or perfectionist way of life; it is one of freedom and love as we pursue every godly principle until it becomes natural and the norm for us.

Living counter to our culture is our assignment and our goal. When you are so sick of living in a sick world—a world that seems determined to continue on a downward spiral of self-destruction—remember this: You don't feel uncomfortable because you *live* in the world, but because you don't *belong* to it. You don't feel pain because you *don't* fit in, but because as a Christian you *can't* fit in.

---

How have you chafed against the world recently?

How have you handled a recent situation differently than you would have months ago?

What irritates you the most about being different?

What do you like the most about it?

What changes do you still have ahead of you in overcoming conformity with the world?

# Chapter · 25 ·

## Eternally

"For God so loved the world that he gave his one and only Son, that whoever believes in him shall not perish but have eternal life."

John 3:16

THE HIGH SCHOOL STUDENT WAILS, "Four whole years? I don't want to go to school anymore. I want to get a job and make some money. When I'm eighteen, I'm getting my own apartment and a life of my own."

How long the years ahead of us seem, and how short the ones behind us. We think in terms of seconds, minutes, days, weeks, months, and years—no wonder it's so difficult to grasp the concept of living eternally.

Living in transition for even a few days or weeks is very difficult for some people. Putting off immediate gratification for a few years of study or training can seem like an unbearable burden.

All through the Scriptures we are reminded that God is forever—not just forever in the future but forever in all that has come before. (See Genesis 1:1.)

It's hard to think of anything existing forever before the world was created when my concept of the world is that it only came into being when I did.

It is much too marvelous to think that God existed, that He worked in lives and that He loved people before me. It's almost inconceivable that He could have answered prayers, intervened in affairs of nations, and wooed people to himself for years and generations before I was ever born.

So when God speaks to us of an eternal perspective, it seems beyond our comprehension. Fortunately, He does not require that we fully comprehend it before we accept it. We don't make facts true by believing them; they are true whether we believe them or not.

God's Word states simply that those who believe in Jesus will have eternal life. He doesn't require that we understand the full implications of eternity—only that we accept His Son, Jesus.

Those who have never known security, who were injured by unstable relationships, have a hard time with promises of the eternal, such as the one contained in John 10:28:

"I give them eternal life, and they shall never perish; no one can snatch them out of my hand."

We don't wait for eternity to begin—eternity has no beginning—it *was* forever and *will be* forever. God had no beginning and has no end. Knowing Him is how we plug into eternity, the means by which we catch hold of something that has no beginning and promises that never end.

"Now this is eternal life: that they may know you, the only true God, and Jesus Christ, whom you have sent" (John 17:3).

Eternal life is a gift of God (Romans 6:23). And, it comes through our Savior and Lord, Jesus Christ.

Knowing Jesus is to experience eternity. This is the promise of God, before the beginning of time, and God doesn't lie (Titus 1:2).

Once I heard that from the earth we only see half of a rainbow. Arching high in the sky, stretching to the horizon it always seemed whole to me. But from the window of an airplane you can look down and see a whole rainbow, perfectly circular, with no beginning and no end.

Eternity is like a rainbow, and from the earth we can see only the part that is not blocked by the horizon of our earthly experiences. The timeless cannot be measured in seconds, minutes, or hours.

Knowing who you are in Christ is your connection to eternity. When we are aware of our eternal life, it gives new perspective to our momentary trials and struggles.

New perspective does not mean that we feel the pain any less, but that there is hope for change. Eternity certainly does seem to give enough time for resolution, or at the very least improvement.

———————

When you are feeling pressured by time, are you more likely to think of the situation in relation to the present moment or in relation to eternity?

When you are struggling and it seems to go on endlessly, what thought patterns could you choose to change—not to minimize the problem, but to maximize your hope?

What truths do you need to tell yourself on a regular basis about who you are in Christ?
Legally:

Relationally:


Spiritually:


Culturally:


Eternally:

Strategy VI

You can become
an overcomer.

Y *ou, dear children, are from God and have overcome them, because the one who is in you is greater than the one who is in the world.*

1 JOHN 4:4

"HOW DO YOU DO IT?" someone once asked me. I'd been through a life-threatening health crisis, and what she really wanted to know was how she could make any sense of the pain and struggle in her own life.

How do we grow through trial? How do any of us survive regret? How do we maintain our hope during distress, or our joy in the very heart of sorrow? *We become overcomers.*

While that sounds simple, it is difficult in practice.

Becoming an overcomer isn't something that is done in classes, but rather in life—right in the middle of the trial, temptation, or testing. It is not done in the absence of trouble, as a work of preparation, but in the face of trouble, when it is the most difficult. An *overcomer* has overcome something; a *victor* has been through a battle; a *conqueror* has defeated an opponent.

Overcomers learn never to ask: "Why me?" Instead, they ask: "How can I grow stronger?" Victors learn to stop whining and start shining their weapons of warfare. Conquerors don't shrink from their opponents; they learn to understand and outmaneuver them.

From all that you have learned in this study so far, I think you can see that to make sense of your pain and struggle, you must decide to commit yourself to *becoming an overcomer.* In my own life, fighting my own battles and struggling with my own pain, I have discovered five guiding principles that have helped me to make and keep my commitment to becoming an overcomer. Like Paul, I do not consider myself as having achieved, but I have found how to receive from God the strength and motivation to keep working on it. Are you willing to work with me?

# Chapter · 26 ·

## Cry Out to the Lord

*"The righteous cry out, and the LORD hears them; he delivers them from all their troubles."*

Psalm 34:17

A LONG TIME AGO I started asking people who were struggling, "Have you cried out to God—or have you simply cried?" It's important that we understand the difference.

I lived all my childhood as a tender, sensitive little girl, otherwise known to my family as a crybaby. I promised myself that as an adult I would no longer be a crybaby. I not only fulfilled that promise, I carried it to an extreme. Working hard to suppress every sensitive emotion eventually left me numb and merciless. For years I didn't shed a tear. One day, life took an unexpected turn.

Everything I wanted, everything I planned, everything I had worked for crumbled to dust around me. Watching the demise of my well-thought-out life overwhelmed me—I collapsed into tears. I didn't cry for just a few minutes, I cried for months.

Stored-up frustrations, disappointments and hurts came gushing out. Spiritually drained, I began to seek the Lord, and finally turned my tears of grief and self-pity into crying out to

God. And in doing so, I discovered the important difference between crying over my losses and crying out to God.

When I cried over my losses, I only slid deeper into my pain. But when I cried out to God, He helped me! He helped me deal with the pain, helped me to see my mistakes, and He helped me to make corrections in my attitudes. Now I firmly believe that if we only cry, we will weep without seeing positive change. But if we cry out to God, our tears can be used to produce within us what He desires for us.

Crying out to God begins with two essential presuppositions: First, we are willing to admit there is a problem; second, we are willing to admit we need to change.

Sometimes we are not willing to admit there is any problem at all. Living in denial we bottle up our tears and suppress our pain. Going about our daily lives, we wonder why relationships seem shallow and cold. We plan exciting activities and make wonderful decisions, but soon we feel bored and emotionally flat. Rather than deal with our numbness, many look for something even more exciting and adventurous—and on and on.

The second presupposition is the willingness to admit we need to change—not a new job, or a new place to live. But a new person within. Perhaps we think our need is for security, fulfillment, position, recognition, appreciation or validation. But inner needs can never be met by material possessions, or by moving to an upper-class neighborhood, or getting a promotion at work.

The Bible shows us how godly men and women cried out to God:

1. *Cry out to God alone.*

"Cry out to God Most High, to God, who fulfills his purpose for me" (Psalm 57:2).

"I cry to you, O LORD; I say, 'You are my refuge, my portion in the land of the living' " (Psalm 142:5).

2. *Cry from the deepest part of your heart and your pain.*

"Out of the depths I cry to you, O LORD" (Psalm 130:1).

3. *Speak of your pain and your need to God.*

"In the morning, O LORD, you hear my voice" (Psalm 5:3).

"I cry aloud to the LORD; I lift up my voice to the LORD for mercy" (Psalm 142:1).

4. *Ask for mercy.*

"The LORD has heard my cry for mercy; the LORD accepts my prayer" (Psalm 6:9).

5. *Ask for help.*

"Listen to my cry for help, my King and my God, for to you I pray" (Psalm 5:2).

6. *Look to Him for shelter.*

"Have mercy on me, O God, have mercy on me, for in you my soul takes refuge. I will take refuge in the shadow of your wings until the disaster has passed" (Psalm 57:1).

7. *Trust God.*

"Let the morning bring me word of your unfailing love, for I have put my trust in you" (Psalm 143:8).

8. *Wait for His response.*

"I lay my requests before you and wait in expectation" (Psalm 5:3).

9. *Rest.*

"My soul finds rest in God alone; my salvation comes from him. He alone is my rock and my salvation; he is my fortress, I will never be shaken" (Psalm 62:1–2).

---

If you were to cry out to God, how would you articulate your problem?

What words would you choose to express your need?

Does the thought of crying out deeply to God frighten you? If so, why?

Why do we hesitate to ask God for shelter and refuge?

Is your level of trust in God deepening? How?

If you were to totally trust God for your life, how would that change how you approach your struggles?

If you were to totally rest, trusting God, how would that change your life?

# Chapter
## · 27 ·

### Living on God's Word

*"How can a young man keep his way pure? By living according to your word."*

Psalm 119:9

BECOMING AN OVERCOMER doesn't end with crying out to God—it begins there. It continues as we live and embrace certain disciplines.

Even in the most difficult of circumstances, disciplines provide a steadying influence. During times of transition disciplines give stability; in seasons of distress, they bring a feeling of normalcy.

The Christian life that is based on God's Word is capsulized in Psalm 119:9–16. If you are really serious about becoming an overcomer, you would do well to pattern your daily disciplines after the ones contained in this wonderful passage:

1. *Seek God with your whole heart.*

"I seek you with all my heart; do not let me stray from your commands" (Psalm 119:10).

Open, with no reservation, is a good definition of *wholehearted.* If I am to seek God with my whole heart, I must check to see if I am willing to be totally open with Him, to totally trust Him—or to admit that I am keeping a little something hidden away, reserved, out of His reach. Maybe it's a secret about myself I don't like. Perhaps it's a pain I am afraid to share with Him, fearing He will tell me it's all my fault. I often sit in my recliner and picture my chest as having doors, like a cupboard. As a visual aid (for myself, not for God), I consciously open those doors and let everything inside me be exposed to God.

I have discovered that if I am to seek God with a whole heart, I need to let Him see *all* that is in me. I bring Him my entire heart—the part that is hurt, the part that is healthy, the part that is doubtful—every part of it.

### 2. Hide His Word in your heart.

"I have hidden your word in my heart that I might not sin against you" (Psalm 119:11).

If my heart represents the inner part of me—the very center of my life, including my thoughts, reactions, and attitudes—then hiding God's Word in my heart is more than just memorizing verses. Hiding His Word in my heart means that I take His Word into the very hidden areas of my life, including those of pain and struggle.

### 3. Remain teachable.

"Praise be to you, O LORD; teach me your decrees" (Psalm 119:12).

If we are not careful, the pain and struggle we live with every day can make us calloused and hard. Looking at every problem with a teachable attitude can help us learn how to become an overcomer. Remaining teachable can seem like a vulnerable way to live. But remember, we can cry out to God from the depths of our being, and we can learn to place our trust in Him. And we can rest.

### 4. Speak of His words and ways.

"With my lips I recount all the laws that come from your mouth" (Psalm 119:13).

I remember asking my Grandpa Sampson why Grandma always kept her flour and sugar in a particular cupboard. "That's just the way she does things," he answered, "and I just go along with it." Grandpa loved Grandma, and he knew her ways. He didn't always understand her ways, but he knew them and respected them.

We may not always understand God's ways. But when we love Him, we accept them, we respect them and we live by them.

5. *Rejoice in God's will.*

"I rejoice in following your statutes as one rejoices in great riches" (Psalm 119:14).

Following God's will and living by His statutes is cause for joy. Living the Christian life is not maximizing what we can't have, but how much we can have. It is not focusing on what is denied but all that is promised.

6. *Meditate on His precepts, consider His ways.*

"I meditate on your precepts and consider your ways" (Psalm 119:15).

I have several pictures of my grandchildren. I look at them frequently. I observe their growth and notice little changes. I examine every detail of their little faces, their shiny hair and miniature hands. I take careful note of their cute mannerisms, remember wonderful conversations I've had with them: I think about them in luxurious excess.

It's much the same with God's precepts. I like finding little obscure phrases in the Bible that contain huge truths, comparing them to other gems I've discovered before. I like to link them together, find a common thread of meaning, and see if there isn't a process or bigger picture of meaning that I can apply to the common areas of my life.

I love following the chain references on a particular topic all the way through the Bible. To me it's like listening to an entire symphony, but picking out only the flute, the violin, or cello line to savor. Little by little, note by note, precept by precept. It is a wonderful mental activity that greatly feeds my spirit.

7. *Read God's Word frequently.*

"I delight in your decrees; I will not neglect your word" (Psalm 119:16).

I have four simple goals for my own devotional reading of the Bible.

*First*: to read it every day.

*Second*: to pay attention—that is, to discipline my mind to observe details such as context, culture, and principles.

*Third*: to learn how to apply it to my own life.

*Fourth*: to act on it.

Making changes in my attitudes, setting personal boundaries, setting priorities, and making decisions are all much more successful if I have maintained my daily meditation in God's Word.

If we are serious about becoming an overcomer, it will require that we live according to God's Word. No matter how tough the day, no matter how much sleep we've lost the night before, God's Word must be our priority. It must become as necessary to our day as taking a trip with a map, or planning a meal using a menu and recipes.

———————

How is your quiet time routine?

What is the hardest part about having a daily quiet time?

Are you able to be totally open with God? If not, why not?

In what ways are you the most teachable?

Name a precept or principle of God's Word that has helped you to make a change in an attitude or a decision.

What makes your daily devotions better for you?

What do you plan to study after you complete this book?

Chapter
· 28 ·

## Walk in Integrity

*"Vindicate me, O LORD, for I have led a blameless life;
I have trusted in the LORD without wavering. Test me,
O LORD, and try me, examine my heart and my mind;
for your love is ever before me, and I walk continually in
your truth."*

Psalm 26:1–3

ANYONE WHO KNOWS ME can tell you that I make more than my share of mistakes. They could also tell you that I'm harder on myself about those mistakes than most people. You see, I want perfection. And for a mere mortal, perfection is an impossible dream.

But not so with *integrity*. Integrity is not only a desirable goal, it is reachable, and it doesn't require perfection.

In the King James Version of the Bible, Psalm 26:1 reads, "I have walked in mine integrity."

Integrity is adhering to a code of personal values that include honesty, openness, and truth.

Does that mean that a person of integrity never cheats on a diet, overlooks an important detail, or weakens in the face of temptation?

No, it means that persons of integrity correct their mis-

141

takes whenever possible, make amends whenever necessary, and repent when they have sinned. Persons of integrity grow from their mistakes and missteps, holding the goal of honesty, openness, and truth ever in the forefront. To be a person of integrity requires that we sacrifice pride and selfish attitudes.

When persons of integrity suffer, they handle the suffering in such a way as to preserve integrity. That means not retaliating, not defending themselves, allowing time for the truth to be revealed. It means resting in God's justice, and allowing difficult situations to be handled by an objective third party.

When my integrity is questioned, I do not seek ways to protect myself. I simply walk in my integrity, and not in my own strength, wisdom, or judgment. I don't rely on a vast vocabulary or an impressive education, but I rely on God. It is not my responsibility to convince anyone of my integrity, only to walk in it.

To impress people by my integrity is not its purpose. We are honest, open, and truthful for God's glory. He changes me, keeps me, comforts me, and guides me.

Persons of integrity, aware of all their shortcomings, prejudices, and failures, pray with the psalmist:

"Test me, O Lord, and try me, examine my heart and my mind. Use every situation in my life to strengthen me and prove me. Look into my heart, Lord, and see that I am totally Yours. Try my reins and see that You are still in control" (Psalm 26:1–2).

The person of integrity also prays:

"Your love is ever before me. I choose to look to You for solutions instead of at the situation and its threats. I will meditate on Your lovingkindness, not on the stresses of the moment. I will discipline myself to keep You ever before me, keeping this obstacle or affliction from overshadowing the work You are doing within me through it.

"I walk continually in Your truth. I accept what You say about me, not what anyone else thinks of me. I cling to Your Word and my position in Christ no matter how awful I feel about myself.

"Your Word is a lamp unto my feet, a light unto my pathway. I choose not to let it be put out.

"In spite of everything I have been, everything I have

done, every doubt I have had, every mistake I have made, I choose to walk in integrity."

---

How do you feel when you are accused of doing something wrong and the accusation is at least partially true?

What would happen if you didn't defend yourself, but simply acknowledged your responsibility and asked what you could do to make things right?

How threatening is that to you and why? If it isn't threatening, why isn't it?

If you were to walk in integrity, what would that do to your perfectionism?

What would it do to your pride?

How would your life be better?

How would being a person of integrity help you to make sense of your struggles?

As a person of integrity, what do the following promises mean to you?
"May integrity and uprightness protect me, because my hope is in you" (Psalm 25:21).

"In my integrity you uphold me and set me in your presence forever" (Psalm 41:12).

# Chapter · 29 ·

# Live in Hope

*"Moses answered the people, 'Do not be afraid. Stand firm and you will see the deliverance the LORD will bring you today. The Egyptians you see today you will never see again. The LORD will fight for you; you need only to be still.''*

Exodus 14:13–14

I KNOW WHAT IT IS to be discouraged. At times I've felt as if I've stumbled through an emotional minefield. I have struggled with my weight, with family responsibilities, with ministry and financial pressures. I have lived through stress that I thought at the time was unbearable and beyond my ability to manage. I've faced family crises, and wondered if I had the strength to fix dinner.

Often my desires go unfulfilled; sometimes normalcy seems an impossible dream; at the worst possible moment, I seem to be misunderstood.

As stress, responsibilities, afflictions, and unmet needs merge together, *discouragement* hits.

But even on the most discouraging of days, if I take the time to quiet myself and turn my heart toward God, I can hear Him say, "Let not your heart be troubled" (John 14:1).

There are so many times that we face fearful circumstances. But the Word of the Lord remains: Stand firm, hold your ground (Psalm 40:2). God offers us the hope of deliverance. We can see it for ourselves, in our very lives and circumstances.

When you are struggling with pain, living a long time with a difficulty—take hope. When you are discouraged, or threatened by the giants you live with and face every day—take courage. You are not in this battle alone. The Lord will fight for you. Even when you think God can't help this time—He can. He can make sense of the most senseless situation—right in the middle of it. And all the while *you* are becoming an overcomer.

———————

What battle would you like the Lord to enter into and take over for you?

What task seems overwhelming to you at the moment?

What desire have you had that seems delayed in its fulfillment?

If you were to believe the promise of Exodus 14:13–14, how would it change the way you cope with your battles, overwhelming tasks, unfulfilled desires?

### Chapter · 30 ·

### Finding the Strength to Go On

*"I took you from the ends of the earth, from its farthest corners I called you. I said, 'You are my servant'; I have chosen you and have not rejected you. So do not fear, for I am with you; do not be dismayed, for I am your God. I will strengthen you and help you; I will uphold you with my righteous right hand."*

Isaiah 41:9–10

WHO AM I? Why am I here? Where am I going? Does my life make any sense at all?

I often feel totally insignificant, a stranger to the vast throngs of people living right around me. Except for a very few close friends, no one really knows me or cares about me.

Except God. He found me in a very out-of-the-way place—a little girl living on top of a desolate hill out in the desert of California. I was a little person that only God knew about, yet He desired me for His design and purpose.

He called me to be His servant. Not a great warrior, but a person willing to serve Him even in obscurity.

And He calls you. Wherever you are, whatever you are doing, He is calling you. In the midst of your pain and struggle, He calls you—to serve, to work, and to do His will.

He calls us from our place far away from Him, to come and live close to Him. From being a nobody, to finding identity in Him and in serving Him.

We are chosen by Him, to be His treasure, not His slave. Not rejected, but accepted by the living, matchless, majestic God and Savior.

No matter what you are going through, it is essential that you remember that God—

    the I Am
        the living God
            the Savior
                the Redeemer
                    the Provider
                        the Healer
                          the Nurturer—

says:

    I am with you
        beside you
            behind you
                and ahead of you.

He also says,

    Don't be discouraged
        depressed
            defeated
                or troubled.

For I am your God:

    You are mine,
        I won't let anyone harm you
            or anything defeat you;

and I am yours,

    I am not a borrowed God
        not a foreign God
            not a stranger to you
                not unaware of your struggle.
                    I am yours, completely.

I will strengthen you

    to carry what I have given you to carry,
        and I will help you.
            I will carry you.

You will not fall
   nor fail;
      I will uphold you
         with my righteous right hand
            with strength
            and wisdom.
   How can we help but trust such a loving Father? How could we not believe in Him? How could we not let Him have His way in our lives? How could we possibly resist giving Him our pain and struggle and let Him make sense of it all?

---

Today, won't you choose to renew your total commitment to trust Him? Will you declare, "He is my God and I am His?"

Write out your commitment of trust.

Write out what your struggle is.

List the things that give you pain.

If you were to combine your commitment of trust, your struggle, and your pain in a prayer, say what would that prayer be?




If God were to answer your prayer right now—today—how would your life change?

## Leader's Notes

### GROUP GUIDELINE SUGGESTIONS

As mentioned at the beginning of this book, if this study is used in a group setting, members should study the five entries of each section throughout the week in preparation for discussion at the weekly meeting. In this way, the material is covered in six weeks. A group may decide to spend more or less time on a given section depending on the needs of the participants. Discussion questions are included at the end of these leader's notes.

A good general group approach to this study is one of personal investigation and shared responses. Discussion questions will help bring out even more insight into application for personal growth.

In the course of covering the material, some very personal areas of a participant's life may be exposed or brought to mind. A leader should not expect, or force, everyone to participate each time. Do encourage even the slightest participation with affirmative comments, regardless of the contribution.

Because this is a responsive study, there are no wrong answers. The nature of the study tends to get to the heart of many emotional issues. Some people in your group may desperately need a listening ear, and a correction from you may discourage them from participating in the discussion, or even keep them from attending the study again. Allow the Holy Spirit to do the correcting and a deep work of patience and sensitivity in you, the leader.

If an individual monopolizes the conversation or goes off on a tangent, very carefully approach that person afterward and ask if you can be of help individually. There may be times during the study when a person may genuinely come to a breakthrough and will draw the attention of the group to herself and her needs exclusively. That would be the exception, however, not the rule.

If someone in your group asks a question, don't take the responsibility upon yourself to have the sole answer. Allow others in the group to contribute, and let your answer be given last.

There are three basic rules that you should strive to keep without fail:

1. *Start and end the study at the time previously arranged and agreed upon.* Everyone is busy. Set your meeting times and stick to them. One and a half hours generally works well for evening groups; daytime groups may wish to meet for a little longer. Actual study discussion should take only a portion of that time. Fellowship and sharing prayer requests helps develop strong bonds within your group. Make time for that to happen.

2. *Begin and end with prayer.* The opening prayer can be a simple offering by one person asking God's blessing on your time together. You may feel the need in your group to have additional time for prayer concerns or needs of the group. (One effective way to handle this is to have everyone write down the name of the person they are concerned for and a very brief statement about the need on a small piece of paper. The slips are put into a basket and redistributed to the group. Each person then offers a sentence prayer concerning the request they have drawn from the basket.) Closing prayers should be centered around the needs that have arisen related to the study and discussion. Bring the meeting to a close with your own prayer.

3. *Involve everyone.* Many of the issues covered in this study

are of a personal nature. Depending on the amount of abuse and misunderstanding your group members have experienced, some may not be ready to discuss the issues they are presently dealing with. However, during the fellowship time, the time of praying for others, and the ongoing study, seek to build trust and encourage participants to open their hearts and share with the group. Find a way to involve even the most reserved person in a way that is comfortable and safe for her.

Discussion times can be rich and rewarding for everyone— that is, everyone who gets to share and discuss. The size of the group somewhat determines the opportunities for sharing. A group of six members is ideal, but it can work with as many as ten. When the group reaches ten, consider the advantages of dividing into smaller groups of three or four for the sharing and discussion time.

## Discussion Questions

*Orientation and Introduction*

You may find it helpful to have an orientation meeting before you begin a group study of this book. Such a meeting will allow members of the group to have an opportunity to look over the book and to prepare for the first discussion and sharing time.

Begin the introductory meeting by reading together *How to Use This Book*. The following questions will help your group members get off to a good start by helping them understand what is expected to be accomplished in the study.

1. Many people have difficulty fitting a daily quiet time into their routine. What are some of the things you have tried? What are some of the ways that have worked for you, and what are some ways that did not work?
2. Everyone experiences a certain amount of pain and struggle in their lives. What are some general areas that can cause us to suffer pain and struggle? (Past abuse, personal sin, family crises, health problems, financial stress, disabilities, moving, changing jobs, death of a friend or family member, church problems, bad habits, etc.)

3. When a person reads a book or embarks on a new study, not every illustration or example exactly fits his or her particular situation and yet may be helpful in some way. Why do you think this is true?
4. Read aloud the introduction to each study section and then ask yourself what some of your expectations are concerning this study.

*Assignments*

Each day for five days before the group meets again, everyone should study and respond to each of the devotional studies in the section to be discussed at the next meeting*

---

*Strategy Number One: Realize your destiny to be an overcomer.*

To begin the first study, read together the introduction to Strategy Number One, and then use the following questions as models or thought-starters for discussion at your meeting.

1. What would your life be without knowing Christ?
2. How do we know God? How can we know Him better?
3. What difference does knowing God make in our lives, our problems, and how we approach them?
4. In what ways are we becoming more like Christ?
5. Does struggle help or hinder that process?
6. Share about a time when you hurt *with* a person in pain.
7. Tell about a time when you witnessed to someone about Christ; what was the result?
8. If you knew you could not fail, what would you attempt?
9. When are you most tempted to quit or give up in your efforts to be an overcomer?
10. How do you find the courage to get up again when you have failed?
11. How are you more aware of your destiny to overcome after these five studies?

---

*The above group guidelines are based on standard group dynamic concepts as well as the models found in the *Lifeguide Bible Studies*, IVP; *Leading Bible Discussions*, by James F. Nyquist and Jack Kuhatschek, IVP; Aglow International Bible Studies; and Overeaters Victorious Leader's Guidelines.

*Strategy Number Two: Set yourself for the long battle.*

Read the introduction to Strategy Number Two together. Why is setting ourselves for the long battle an unpopular idea?

1. Have you ever, or do you ever use the "baby Christian" excuse?
2. Why are excuses counterproductive?
3. What is the hardest part about becoming mature?
4. When are you the most impatient with yourself and your growth process?
5. What excites you the most: being a victorious, triumphant Christian or becoming an overcomer? What's the difference?
6. Comment on the following:
   - Offering sacrifices of praise
   - Learning to be still
   - Walking in His ways
   - Hanging on to hope
   - Trusting in God
   - Speaking truth to yourself
   - Entering into worship
7. How hard is it for you to wait? Why do you think that is so?
8. What emotional signals do people send when they don't want to wait?
9. How else could you learn patience other than by waiting?
10. Does "fixing your mind" help or hinder the patient waiting process?
11. In what ways have you set yourself for the long battle?

*Strategy Number Three: Understand the obstacles.*

Read the introduction to Strategy Number Three together. What obstacles are you facing at the moment?

1. Share about a time when a dead end became a new beginning.
2. What issue have you tried to avoid with God?

3. Tell about a blind-alley/new-revelation experience you have had.
4. When did you ever get a second chance?
5. Sometimes the very thing we trip over teaches us the most and stumbling blocks become stepping stones. Share about such a lesson in your life.
6. Why is it so hard to see opportunities in obstacles?
7. Why is it so easy to see obstacles in every opportunity?
8. Tell about an experience in which you chose betterness instead of bitterness.

---

*Strategy Number Four: Identify your afflictions.*

Read the introduction to Strategy Number Four together. Who do we usually think of as being afflicted? What are you dealing with that could be defined as trouble or pain that is lasting a long time?

1. What are some of the "personal hell" situations that you know people struggle with?
2. Have you ever felt as if you were a victim of the "Magdalene Malady?" When? Why?
3. In what ways are we most likely to be assaulted by the Devil?
4. Are the assaults always obvious?
5. Share one of your responses to Psalm 34.
6. Share a recent victory.
7. Name a time that you were overwhelmed by circumstances—a "Mara Misery."
8. How is Jesus our Boaz?
9. Who is our Kinsman Redeemer?
10. Are you a do-it-yourselfer?
11. Which is harder? Waiting for God to work things out, or taking things into our own hands?
12. What results can we expect from each?
13. What is the major contributor to "Leah Legacy" afflictions?
14. Whom do you know who lives with a caregiver's challenge? How can you help?

15. What thread of thought runs through each affliction written about in the study, and how can you apply the truth here to your own situation?

--------

*Strategy Number Five: Know who you are in Christ.*

Read the introduction to Strategy Number Five together. If in Christ we are made different, victorious and new, why do we have to read and study about it? Why aren't we changed automatically if we are identified with Christ?

1. Whose name have you been given the legal right to use?
2. Is it possible to abuse the use of Christ's name? Tell about a time when you felt you witnessed such an abuse.
3. Knowing we can have free access to God is wonderful, but do we always take that freedom? Why, or why not?
4. Chapter 22 gave us pictures of being a child of God in human concepts. Is it easy or difficult for you to think of climbing up on God's lap and having Him reach into a pocket to give you a treasure? Why, or why not?
5. Chapter 23 listed ten points to help navigate difficulties. Which one did you find the most helpful and why?
6. What does living in a new dimension mean to you?
7. We are different when we are in Christ. In what ways are we different from before we knew Christ? In what ways are we different from our world's culture?
8. Eternity is a difficult concept. How do you handle the concept of forever?
9. When your struggles seem to go on endlessly, what thought patterns could you choose to change—not to minimize the problem, but to maximize hope?
10. Finish this statement: In Christ I am _____ .

--------

*Strategy Number Six: You can become an overcomer.*

Read the introduction to Strategy Number Six together. What is the hardest part to becoming an overcomer? What is the most rewarding part of becoming an overcomer?

1. When you are struggling, are you more likely to cry out to God or suppress your pain?
2. How does the biblical pattern for crying out to God help you?
3. What area of discipline is most difficult for you?
4. How do studies like this one help you sustain the discipline of a daily quiet time?
5. What is the hardest part about having a daily quiet time?
6. Are you able to be totally open with God? When is it the easiest? Hardest?
7. Define integrity.
8. What does it mean to walk honestly before God in integrity?
9. How do you feel when you are accused of doing something wrong and the accusation is at least partially true?
10. What would happen if you didn't defend yourself, but simply acknowledged your responsibility and asked what you could do to make it right?
11. If you were to believe the promise of Exodus 14:13–14, how would it change the way you cope with your struggle?
12. How has this study helped you to find the strength to go on?
13. In what areas have you changed your prayers from requests for deliverance from struggle, to requests for strength to be an overcomer?
14. Share what you have been able to overcome by being a part of this group study.